T0307837

LITERARY CINCINNATI

LITERARY
CINCINNATI

THE MISSING CHAPTER

DALE PATRICK BROWN

OHIO UNIVERSITY PRESS
ATHENS, OHIO
In association with the
MERCANTILE LIBRARY
CINCINNATI, OHIO

Ohio University Press, Athens, Ohio 45701
ohioswallow.com

© 2011 by Ohio University Press
All rights reserved

To obtain permission to quote, reprint, or otherwise reproduce or distribute
material from Ohio University Press publications, please contact our rights and
permissions department at (740) 593-1154 or (740) 593-4536 (fax).

Printed in the United States of America
Ohio University Press books are printed on acid-free paper ⊗™

20 19 18 17 16 15 14 13 12 11   5 4 3 2 1

Library of Congress Cataloging-in-Publication Data

Brown, Dale Patrick.
 Literary Cincinnati : the missing chapter / Dale Patrick Brown.
    p. cm.
 Summary: "The history of Cincinnati runs much deeper than the stories of hogs
that once roamed downtown streets. In addition to hosting the nation's first
professional baseball team, the Tall Stacks river boat celebration, and the May
Festival, there's another side to the city—one that includes some of the most
famous names and organizations in American letters. Literary Cincinnati fills in this
missing chapter, taking the reader on a joyous ride with some of the great literary
personalities who have shaped life in the Queen City. Meet the young Samuel
Clemens working in a local print shop, Fanny Trollope struggling to open her
bizarre bazaar, Sinclair Lewis researching Babbitt, hairdresser Eliza Potter telling the
secrets of her rich clientele, and many more who defined the nineteenth- and early
twentieth-century Queen City. For lovers of literature everywhere—but especially
in Cincinnati—this is a literary tour that will entertain, inform, and amuse." —
Provided by publisher.
 Includes bibliographical references and index.
 ISBN 978-0-8214-1969-4 (hardback)
 1. Literary landmarks—Ohio—Cincinnati. 2. Authors, American—Homes and
haunts—Ohio—Cincinnati. 3. Cincinnati (Ohio)—Intellectual life. 4. City and
town life in literature. 5. Cincinnati (Ohio)—In literature. I. Title.
 PS255.C56B76 2011
 810.9'977178—dc23
                            2011027224

To Lou

CONTENTS

ILLUSTRATIONS

PREFACE

It looked like rain on the morning of April 27, 1882, but it turned out to be a beautiful day, and a crowd estimated at between twenty-five and fifty thousand people, many of them schoolchildren, flocked to what had once been Nicholas Longworth's vineyards in Cincinnati's Eden Park. Even a serious runaway buggy accident couldn't mar the occasion. Flags flew, worthies spoke, and thirteen guns saluted.

That grand nineteenth-century occasion, Ohio's first Arbor Day, was the highlight of the American Forestry Congress held in Cincinnati that week.[1] Much of the inspiration, hard work, and leadership for the day came from Cincinnati school superintendent John B. Peaslee, a man so devoted to the pursuit of literary endeavors that he had already established local celebrations of the birthdays of Henry Wadsworth Longfellow and Oliver Wendell Holmes. For Arbor Day, Peaslee saw to it that an Authors Grove was among the several groves planted.

That first year, thirty-five seedlings were planted in Authors Grove near the spot where Eden Park's historic water tower stands today. Cincinnati schoolchildren selected the authors to be honored, and in later years other memorial trees were added. Granite markers, paid for by the children, were placed at the bases of the trees.

In the fall of 1980, almost a hundred years after the original event and some ten years before I moved to Cincinnati, the city's Board of Park Commissioners realized that Authors Grove was gradually slipping away. The stone markers were deteriorating, and tree roots were displacing some of them. The park staff recovered what they could of the markers, about forty-five in all, and embedded them in a curved brick wall with columns near the original site, adding a commemorative plaque and a sculpture. And there, with the names of Washington Irving, T. Buchanan Read, Ralph Waldo Emerson,

Nathaniel Hawthorne, George Elliston, Alice Cary, and many others, it stood, a lasting testimony to Cincinnati's literary interests.

Except that it doesn't exist today. A granite book rests on one of the 1980 columns, and informational plaques about the groves have been installed, but the crumbling stones, considered a mowing obstacle and a drain on the budget, were removed in 2009 and put into storage. There are no plans to reinstall them.

If the public has noticed the change, it has remained silent.

In some ways, Authors Grove is an apt metaphor for Cincinnati's literary history. During the nineteenth century, even as early as 1828, when Fanny Trollope came to town, Cincinnati had many literary devotees, including both readers and writers. Several noteworthy authors got their start in the city during that period, and organizations such as the Young Men's Mercantile Library Association and the Literary Club of Cincinnati thrived. In fact, the city can point to an impressive literary history, but it rarely does. Instead visitors hear about chili, soap, the fine arts, May Festival, machine tools, Porkopolis, and the Red Stockings, the nation's first professional baseball team. No one thinks of Cincinnati in literary terms, even though to tell the tale of literary Cincinnati is, in many respects, to tell the tale of Cincinnati itself. Cincinnati may once have been the Athens of the West, but if the written word was part of that, it has slipped through the cracks of time.

To be fair, there is considerable literary activity in the city today, unheralded though it might be. The Mercantile (now the Mercantile Library of Cincinnati) celebrated its 175th anniversary in 2010 with a strong, well-attended season of events. Book clubs proliferate, and the city operates one of the best public library systems in the country. There are also a popular annual book fair (Books by the Banks), a plethora of sponsored talks by notable authors, writers groups, and classes.

I harbor a lifelong interest in all things literary, so I readily admit to bias, but I believe Cincinnati's literary history is deserving of greater attention. Without Harriet Beecher Stowe's years in Cincinnati, would she have written her seminal *Uncle Tom's Cabin*? If Lafcadio Hearn had not served his apprenticeship on Cincinnati newspapers, would he have developed the skills to introduce the world to Japan? Would McGuffey's *Readers* have become some of the nation's most influential publications if a Cincinnati printer had not commissioned and promoted them? You can judge for yourself, but I think not.

In this book I have tried to consider how Cincinnati's literary figures have played their parts in both history and literature. My choices are personal and heavily influenced by space considerations, with apologies to the legacies of anyone I have omitted. I especially regret not being able to cover Stephen Foster (1826–1864), the well-known songwriter, who spent four years in the city; Charles Cist (1792–1868), editor and historian; Henry Howe (1816–1893), author of the important *Historical Collections of Ohio*; William Henry Venable (1836–1920), author and teacher of note; and Benjamin Drake (1794–1841), editor and author of *The Great Indian Chief of the West; Or Life and Adventures of Black Hawk*. And then there were the visits of Alexis de Tocqueville (1831), Oscar Wilde (1882), Sir Arthur Conan Doyle (1894), Alfred Noyes (1941) . . . the list goes on.

I also wish I could have spent more time writing about African Americans with Cincinnati literary connections. Black leaders in the city have historically tended to focus on education, civil rights, and social activism rather than on endeavors that might strictly be called "literary," but journalist Wendell P. Dabney (1865–1952), who edited the *Union* for more than forty years; historian George Washington Williams (1849–1891), who wrote what is considered to be the first history of African Americans, and educator Peter H. Clark (1829–1925), author of *The Black Brigade of Cincinnati*, would have made excellent subjects

It would be misleading to say that this book is either pure history or pure literary criticism. While I have reflected on writing accomplishments and historical context, I have focused primarily on telling stories, tales of real flesh-and-blood people who lived and worked in the region. The men and women featured here have come alive for me, with all their foibles, their achievements, and their everyday problems. Their stories may have lain dormant for decades in dusty, forgotten books and outdated newspapers, but they aren't gone. With a little digging, and occasionally an exploratory walk through our streets, they can be recovered, at least to a degree. I hope my heroes can step off the pages and take their rightful places in the regional consciousness. Trees and stones die or crumble, but words, and the people who write them, need not.

ACKNOWLEDGMENTS

I am indebted to many people for assistance with this book, a cornucopia of details that would have been impossible to put together without them. Unfortunately, some of them will have to go nameless: librarians at the Public Library of Cincinnati and Hamilton County who patiently corrected microfilm snafus or searched out books and documents I couldn't do without; the staff at Spring Grove Cemetery who helped track down hard-to-locate cemetery plots; and quite a few skillful individuals who ushered me through the often cumbersome photo permission process. (Their institutions are acknowledged separately.)

Among others to whom I am grateful are Giovanni Ranieri and his exceptional staff at the Queen City Club, who, not once but several times, graciously pulled out decades of club records so I could search for information on Sinclair Lewis; Steve Schuckman, Jim Burkhardt, Julie Horne, and Vicki Newell with Cincinnati Parks, who enabled me to trace the history of Authors Grove; and Dorothy Lingg, Helen Steiner Rice archivist at the Cincinnati Museum Center, who took the time to check my Rice facts.

And imagine my surprise and gratitude when I went to the James A. Ramage Civil War Museum in Fort Wright, Kentucky, in search of information on William Hooper, and staffer Kathleen Romero offered to lend me the beautifully assembled scrapbook she had already compiled about him. Thanks also to Adrienne Cowden with the City of Cincinnati, who spent a considerable amount of time in what turned out to be a fruitless search for a painting by T. Buchanan Read.

I also wish to acknowledge *Cincinnati Magazine*, where my stories on the Elliston lectures and Robert Frost first appeared. Linda Vaccariello, executive editor, was invaluable in those efforts.

I am grateful to the many individuals I interviewed for those pieces, and would particularly like to thank Damaris Ames, who took the trouble of copying pages from her father's handwritten journal for me; Pat Ford, who provided a photo from the Berryman days; and the anonymous librarian at the University of Cincinnati Library who pointed me in the direction of Raymond Walters's unpublished journal.

I also owe a huge debt to the Mercantile Library of Cincinnati. Not only have I reprised some of the stories the library published in my earlier book, *Brilliance and Balderdash,* but I have relied upon staff support for photos (thank you, Chris Messick and Cedric Rose) and executive director Albert Pyle's good counsel on all sorts of things, including an extremely helpful first reading of the manuscript.

Other first readers to whom I am deeply indebted are Trudy Backus, volunteer coordinator of Architreks Walking Tours; my wonderful friends Russ and Sydney Schnurr; and my husband Lou Enzweiler, all of whom caught errors and made suggestions that vastly improved the work. Lou also provided logistical, technical, and microfilm support, cheerfully ignoring the fact that I don't know east from west on field trips and couldn't tell a 300 DPI picture from an Etch A Sketch drawing.

Finally, I offer special thanks to David Sanders, Kevin Haworth, Gillian Berchowitz, Nancy Basmajian, Beth Pratt, John Morris, and all the staff at Ohio University Press. It has been a pleasure to work with them.

CHAPTER ONE

A TROLLOPE! A TROLLOPE!

The most notorious woman in Cincinnati's literary history, indeed arguably the most notorious woman in America in her day, arrived at the city's public landing on February 10, 1828, a total unknown. The short, plump, bright-faced Englishwoman with Saxon coloring, Frances (Fanny) Trollope, along with two daughters, a manservant, and a young Frenchman, disembarked the steamboat *Criterion* from Memphis, found a hotel, and set in motion a tale that some say affects the city to this day.

In 1828, Cincinnati was booming. Although it had been founded only forty years earlier, the population had already grown to about twenty thousand. Immigrants were pouring in, and commerce was strong. Indeed, it was Cincinnati's reputation as the country's fastest-growing city that drew Trollope. She and her family (she had a husband and three other children back in England) were facing financial ruin; she needed money.[1]

The forty-nine-year-old Trollope had come to America less than two months earlier, when her social reformer friend Fanny Wright asked her to join her "experiment," a settlement known as Nashoba in the backwoods near Memphis. Wright's plan was to purchase slaves and set them to work building a new community to pay back their purchase price. After that, they would be given free passage out of the country.[2]

Artist Auguste Hervieu, an exile from monarchist France who was the Trollope children's drawing teacher, came along on the

FIGURE I.I Fanny Trollope, engraving by Joseph Brown. *Cincinnati Museum Center–Cincinnati Historical Society Library*

American excursion as drawing master for Nashoba. Both he and Trollope, however, were horrified at the primitive conditions they found. They quickly resolved to flee to Cincinnati and appealed to Nashoba for a $300 loan to make the trip.

Trollope's initial impression of Cincinnati was positive. She described the city in an early letter as a "remote but very pretty nest." The weather was dreary, but "the country beautiful, and wonderful in its rapid progress towards the wealth and the wisdom, the finery and the folly of the Old World; and I like it well," she said.[3] However, there was one unpleasant episode almost immediately: her innkeeper berated her for having the audacity to ask for tea in her room.[4]

The Trollope party quickly moved out of the hotel into a rented house on Race Street near the center of town.[5] Unfortunately, the new place proved unsatisfactory too. Trollope had failed to notice that there was no drain, pump, or cistern for the house, and no way to dispose of garbage. When she inquired of the landlord what to do about the garbage, he told her to put it in the middle of the road for the hogs, which roamed everywhere. Mrs. Trollope, who had little appreciation for Cincinnati's status as the hog capital of the world, was simply shocked. She grew even more outraged when the hogs nuzzled her hands as she walked about town.[6]

Trollope had sent her sixteen-year-old son Henry to an Indiana school when she left Memphis, but that became a problem as well. The school advertised a work/study program, but there was more work than study, and Henry got ill. Trollope had to borrow money from Hervieu to bring her son to Cincinnati. Soon Hervieu became her complete financial support, because Mr. Trollope did not answer her desperate pleas for money. She frantically searched for a solution, and one of her first ideas was to put Henry, who was by then recovering, to work giving Latin lessons. Mrs. Trollope ran an advertisement in the March 28, 1828, edition of the *Cincinnati Gazette* seeking fifty cents an hour for his services.

Meanwhile, Hervieu started a drawing school and began painting on the side.[7]

The Trollopes moved once again after Henry joined them, this time to a rented cottage in a community known as Mohawk, about a mile and a half from downtown on the corner of Dunlop Street and McMicken Avenue (until 1870 this was Hamilton Road).[8] According to Fanny's son Tom, who later visited from England, the new place was "a roomy, bright-looking house, built of wood, and all white with the exception of the green Venetian blinds. It stood in its own 'grounds,' but these grounds consisted of a large field, uncultivated save for a few potatoes in one corner of it."[9] Known as Gano Lodge, it proved to be a better home for the Trollopes, but problems still plagued them. Hogs, those infernal hogs, were fed and lodged there; then a new slaughterhouse opened nearby, putting dead animals in close proximity to what otherwise would have been pretty streams.

Mrs. Trollope also discovered that her new neighbors tended to drop in without notice, conducting what she considered boorish conversation in displays of "violent intimacy."[10]

Mrs. Trollope did make a few friends in Cincinnati and was entertained at least a few times. For example, the former proprietor of Egyptian Hall, a London museum, threw a dinner party in her honor in northern Kentucky shortly after her arrival. And she held at least one dinner party herself, entertaining about a hundred guests with theatricals and dancing.[11] However, with little money and no local contacts, she was hardly cutting a large figure in Cincinnati society. She had brought no letters of introduction to the city, an oversight that proved grave. She finally requested one from the marquis de Lafayette, who had previously visited Cincinnati and was an acquaintance through Fanny Wright, but his letter failed to arrive in time to help.[12]

One new friend did prove fortuitous. Joseph Dorfeuille, a New Orleans naturalist, was the curator of the Western Museum at the corner of Main and Columbia Streets. Filled with objects Cincinnatians found of little interest—Indian artifacts, minerals, and fossils—the museum was attracting few visitors. Dorfeuille ordered wax figures to spur business and hired a young assistant named Hiram Powers to repair those that arrived damaged. Mrs. Trollope hit it off with Powers immediately and came up with an idea for a new attraction. It was called "Invisible Girl" and featured Henry Trollope as an oracle. Some of Hervieu's artwork was included as well.[13]

"Invisible Girl" was such a success that Hervieu, Mrs. Trollope, and Powers, who later became one of the best-known sculptors of the nineteenth century, tackled another exhibit suggested by Mrs. Trollope. Taking its inspiration from Dante's *Divine Comedy*, it was known as "Infernal Regions."[14] Mrs. Trollope wrote a four-page program featuring quotations she translated from Dante, as well as what her son Tom later described as "explanations of the author's meaning, and descriptions in very bugaboo style, and in every variety of type, with capitals of every sort of size, of all the horrors of the supposed scene."[15] "Infernal Regions" was a triumph. It ran for more than twenty-five years and is credited with saving the museum from extinction. It still exists today, as part of the Cincinnati Museum Center at Union Terminal.[16]

At some point, probably after her husband and son arrived for a visit late in 1828, Mrs. Trollope conceived her grandest money-making scheme yet. She had become convinced that there was a market for fancy goods and a need for entertainment venues in the bustling city. She had observed that Cincinnatians didn't play billiards or cards, didn't put on concerts or dinner parties, and rarely attended theatrical performances.[17] She thought them, in fact, the dullest people she had ever met and reasoned that they could use some fun. She would build a structure to house a bazaar for upscale goods, a coffeehouse, an "elegant Saloon" for refreshments, a bar room, an exhibition gallery, a ballroom, and a place for panoramic exhibitions.[18] By January of 1829, she and her husband had purchased land for the project, and Mr. Trollope had agreed to return to England to raise money for it.[19]

Mrs. Trollope contracted malaria and almost died in the summer of 1829, but the bazaar went up anyway. Situated on Third Street east of Broadway, near the site of old Fort Washington, it was designed by Seneca Palmer and was without question the most unusual building ever built in Cincinnati.[20] Mrs. Trollope, a romantic at heart, wanted to make a statement to attract attention, and so she did. The four-story structure, sometimes considered the first department store, most closely resembled the Egyptian Revival style, but was actually something of a hodgepodge in design. Timothy Flint, editor of the *Western Monthly Review* and one of the few people Trollope liked in Cincinnati, described it as a "queer, unique, crescented Turkish Babel."[21] Urgently in need of money, Trollope pushed up the opening before construction was finished and invited the public to visit on October 16, 1829. Cincinnatians were not impressed, with either the goods or the design. Nor did they like the smell. Trollope's innovative plan to provide lighting with gas, possibly for the first time in the city, went awry, and the bazaar smelled like rotten eggs. She ran an ad to announce that she had switched to oil and spermaceti, but people stayed away anyway.[22]

Mrs. Trollope was also disappointed in the knickknacks, furniture, stationery, china, and so forth that her husband had sent for the bazaar in lieu of money. To make matters worse, she had failed to notice that her offerings were already available in other shops at cheaper prices and that her location, apart from the main shopping area, wasn't the best. And, of course, she hadn't really connected with the city's leading citizens, who might have made the place a success. Yet, she persevered. She presented two evenings of a "Musical Fantasia," but audiences were slim. Hervieu exhibited a massive painting, *The Landing of Lafayette at Cincinnati*, but no luck. By early March 1830, financial disaster had struck. The goods of the bazaar, as well as Mrs. Trollope's personal belongings, were seized

FIGURE 1.2 Trollope's Bazaar on Third Street. *Cincinnati Museum Center– Cincinnati Historical Society Library*

by creditors, and Mrs. Trollope and party were thrown out of their house. A neighbor took them in briefly, but soon they boarded the *Lady Franklin* to get out of town.[23]

Fanny Trollope is believed to have had a travel book in mind from the beginning. Such books were popular at the time, and she kept voluminous notes toward that possible end. She began keeping notes on Cincinnati early in her stay, and three notebooks with some sixty-four thousand words on her American experience are now in the Lilly Library of Indiana University at Bloomington.[24] After she fled the city, she decided she should see other parts of America to broaden her perspective, so she briefly visited Washington, Philadelphia, Virginia, New York, and Niagara Falls. She also stayed for a while with a friend in Maryland. By the time she returned to England in August of 1831, her manuscript was almost done.

When *Domestic Manners of the Americans* came out in 1832, the English, curious about life in America and wrestling with the question of whether to institute greater democracy themselves, devoured the book.[25] Of course, Americans read it too, appalled at their depiction as rude, spitting, bumpkins who lived in a land filled with freewheeling hogs and nasty mosquitoes. The term "to trollopize" was coined to suggest harsh criticism. A man who failed to sit with proper decorum in his theater box or spat on the floor of the music hall was hailed with "A Trollope! A Trollope!"[26] Mrs. Trollope was scorned everywhere in America.

With almost half of *Domestic Manners* specifically focused on Cincinnati, its residents were particularly upset. Cincinnati's self-image and its public image, both of which had been strong when Mrs. Trollope arrived, were seriously damaged. The local citizenry, who thought Mrs. Trollope the rude one, lashed out in anger. Historians have sometimes argued that the book had a positive effect on Cincinnati because it prompted the city to improve its cultural offerings (they are now considered excellent), but Mrs. Trollope's notoriety lives on. As recently as 2003, noted author and literary critic Edmund White, a native Cincinnatian, published *Fanny: A Fiction,* a historical novel that assumes the voice of Mrs. Trollope to tell what purports to be the story of Fanny Wright. The fictional Trollope lapses extensively into tales of her own life, and there, with some embellishments, it all is again: the bazaar, the Western Museum, the hogs, the crude Cincinnati manners. Fortunately, White at least lets poor Hervieu off the hook. Cincinnatians had always gossiped about his relationship with Trollope, but it was probably innocent. White gives her a clandestine affair with an African American blacksmith named Cudjo instead.

Domestic Manners comes off today as somewhat mild, probably truthful, often comic, and in some ways predictable, given that Cincinnati was still a frontier city and that the English and American cultures of the day were so different. Nor is it surprising that Mrs. Trollope, who had miserable experiences in the city, found little to her liking except the meat and vegetables. On the contrary, as one writer pointed out, it is something of a backhanded compliment that she compared a frontier town in its infancy to the great old capitals of Europe.[27]

Fanny Trollope went on to write forty more books, including four novels in which she drew upon her travels in America. One, *The Old World and the New,* features a family not unlike her own that settles on an estate about ten miles from Cincinnati. That book looks more gently at the area, but is rarely read today and never eclipsed the picture she first painted. Although Mrs. Trollope endured other difficult periods—financial struggles, the death of her husband in 1834, and the deaths of three of her five adult children from tuberculosis—she never gave up and ended her life in luxury, living in a Florence mansion called Villa Trollope with her son Tom and his family. Her son Anthony, whose work is said to owe a debt to hers, became one of the Victorian era's most respected authors, and she herself is credited not only with one of the earliest successful writing careers for women but also with influencing the writing of Charles Dickens, Harriet Beecher Stowe, Elizabeth Gaskell, William Makepeace Thackeray, and Charlotte Brontë.[28] She is even given kudos in the art world. She maintained her friendship with Hiram Powers in Europe and encouraged him to branch out from parlor busts into more imaginative work.[29] She died on October 6, 1863, at the age of eighty-four.

Trollope's bazaar was sold to wealthy local arts patron Nicholas Longworth in 1834 and was acquired by the Ohio Mechanics Institute in 1839. The OMI moved out in 1843, and, in the years ahead, "Trollope's Folly" housed a dancing school, medical school, female medical college, hydropathical establishment, convalescent home for federal soldiers, and even a house of prostitution. It was demolished in 1881.[30]

CHAPTER TWO

BUCKEYES, SEMI-COLONS, AND OTHER LITERATI

Fanny Trollope didn't know it, but there were quite a few
cultured people in Cincinnati even as the hogs roamed the
unpaved streets. The first newspaper was established as early as
1793, and before *Domestic Manners* was so much as a scribbled note
in Fanny's notebook, educated settlers from the East were reading the news, importing books, writing and publishing their own
books, opening bookstores, creating literary journals, and founding libraries, schools, and museums.[1] At about the same time Mrs.
Trollope and her party were scrambling to get out of town ahead of
the bill collectors, several genteel groups of educated citizens were
organizing literary gatherings around the city. Those organizations
nurtured the written word in Cincinnati for more than ten of its
formative years, allowing quite a few writers of note to begin their
writing careers or hone their skills.

One of the best-known early organizations was the Semi-Colon
Club. No one knows whether it was established in 1829 or 1830,
who organized it, or what exactly prompted its formation, but one
member, John Parsons Foote, Harriet Beecher Stowe's uncle, later
wrote that the founders were transplanted New Englanders led by
the Reverend E. B. Hall and his wife; Timothy Walker, a prominent
local judge; and Nathan Guilford, a lawyer, author, and advocate
for public education.[2] Another member, Edwin Cranch, said that
newspaper editor Benjamin Drake was instrumental, and Drake's
famous brother, Dr. Daniel Drake, may have been as well. Whoever

was responsible, the organization grew to include many illustrious figures and was a significant factor not only in Cincinnati's cultural development but in the intellectual history of the American West. Progressively for its day, the club included both men and women.[3]

The Semi-Colon Club may have taken its name from the punctuation mark, but another theory says it was based on the idea that the person who provides a new pleasure is entitled to half the praise accorded the discoverer of a new continent. Under that reasoning, a club offering the pleasure of social and intellectual life was entitled to half the praise of the discoverer of America, Christopher Columbus, or *Colon* in Spanish. The latter theory seems a stretch, but whatever the origin of the name, it was memorable, and it stuck.[4]

The club was focused on the reading of short works, usually about four pages, written by participants. It met every two weeks during the winter months, sometimes at the downtown home of William Greene, a distinguished former Rhode Islander, or that of his neighbor Charles Stetson, but more often at the Third and Vine Street mansion of Samuel Foote, another of Stowe's uncles. Simple refreshments—tea, coffee, wine, sandwiches, cake—were served, and then Greene, who was known for his stateliness and his strong reading voice, read the papers to the group. The women sometimes knitted as they listened, and occasionally there were musical entertainments or dancing. Adjournment came early.[5]

According to Cranch, anonymity was critical for the participants of the Semi-Colon Club because it gave "additional freedom to mature writers, while it emboldened beginners to a spontaneity of thought and style, which certainly added to the literary budget of the night." Participants slipped their compositions to the hostess ahead of time or after they arrived for the evening, and there was much conjecture about who wrote what. Authors sometimes confided their identities to their closest friends, and lapses of other sorts occurred. For example, Cranch illustrated his work with pencil sketches that were easily recognizable.[6] Ultimately, quite a few of the papers were published in local newspapers and magazines as well as in national journals.

Topics ranged widely. There were essays on the advantages of traveling by steamboat, and there was a light defense of enthusiasm. There were also humorous pieces, political commentary, doggerel verse, insignificant writings on love, and jokes. Although assessments by modern scholars are not all favorable, the club developed a strong reputation and attracted important visitors when they happened to be in the area.

More than a dozen of the club members were already or would become influential in American literary history, including James H. Perkins, newspaper editor and author of *Annals of the West;* James Freeman Clarke, minister and editor; Timothy Flint, magazine editor; Judge James C. Hall, author and editor of the *Western Monthly Magazine;* and Joseph Longworth, arts patron and son of Cincinnati's wealthy Nicholas Longworth. Others were Ormsby M. Mitchel, prominent astronomer and Civil War general; Edward D. Mansfield, author and editor of the *Cincinnati Chronicle;* three Misses Blackwell, including Elizabeth, who became the first female doctor in the United States; and Carolyn Lee Hentz, novelist.[7] The most famous members were the Beechers and the Stowes: Harriet Beecher and her future husband, biblical scholar Calvin Stowe; Harriet's father, the prominent Presbyterian minister Lyman Beecher; and her sister, Catharine, a leader in education.

The Semi-Colon Club flourished for a number of years until it ceased to exist sometime between 1837 and 1846. The financial crisis of 1837, which caused Samuel Foote to lose his beautiful home and the club to lose its most popular meeting place, may have been the fatal stroke, although the group continued to publish a magazine until the mid-1840s.

About the same time the Semi-Colon Club was organized, the Cincinnati Literary Society was established. It seems to have included only men, but, like the Semi-Colon Club, it focused on

FIGURE 2.1 Harriet Beecher Stowe by Walter Driesbach. *Courtesy of the Mercantile Library of Cincinnati*

FIGURE 2.2 Daniel Drake, as shown in *Memoirs of the Life and Services of Daniel Drake* by Edward D. Mansfield, 1855

stimulating literary and intellectual endeavors. It met on Friday nights and featured both debates and the reading of essays. Some of the city's most cultured people were members, including Judge Hall, a president of the Cincinnati Chamber of Commerce and also a member of the Semi-Colon Club; Charles D. Drake, son of Dr. Daniel Drake; and Major James F. Conover, editor and owner of the *Cincinnati Daily Whig.*

The Cincinnati Literary Society initially had a meeting room in a building on the corner of Main and Fifth Streets, where it assembled a collection of books. After incorporation by the Ohio legislature in 1834, it moved to other quarters. Members of the group were assigned the writing of essays in alphabetical order by name, but apparently essays were of less interest than debates. When a member failed to fulfill his writing commitment, which occurred with some regularity, a fine was levied. Nevertheless, the club was strong enough that it eventually rented rooms from the Young Men's Mercantile Library Association on Walnut Street and met on and off for about ten years. It ended in February of 1840.[8]

For Dr. Daniel Drake, participating in the Semi-Colon Club was hardly his only literary activity. "I was molded to do many things," he said, and he was right. He has sometimes been called the "Franklin of Cincinnati."[9] Born in 1785 in Plainfield, New Jersey, he came with his parents to Maysville, Kentucky, several years later, about the time Cincinnati was founded.[10] He was only fifteen when he crossed into Ohio to study medicine with a Cincinnati physician. Not content with the typical apprenticeship of the day, he decided to extend his education at the University of Pennsylvania and eventually became the first Ohio resident to receive a medical degree. His professional career included establishing an active medical practice, helping to found the second medical school west of the Alleghenies (the Medical College of Ohio), founding an eye hospital and a commercial hospital, and editing one of the earliest medical journals in the West. He also published several important medical and scientific treatises.[11]

Drake was instrumental in founding several organizations that promoted the intellectual and educational development of the Cincinnati area. Among them were the Lancaster Seminary, which later merged into Cincinnati College; the Western Museum (the one Fanny Trollope saved); the School of Literature and Arts, an organization that encouraged intellectual activity; and an early circulating library. And his writings were not limited to medical topics. Some of his books and pamphlets, such as *Natural and Statistical View, or Picture of Cincinnati and the Miami Country*,[12] describe the region's natural and social history and are considered critical to an understanding of the early years of the city.

Drake married, but his wife died in 1825, leaving him the single parent of a son and two daughters. In 1833, at least in part to forward his daughters' social education and finishing, he decided to take another step for literary Cincinnati: he established regular evening soirees at his Vine Street home.[13]

Drake is said to have patterned his parties after social evenings he had attended at the home of the scientist Caspar Wistar in Philadelphia.[14] He had always been fond of "rational amusement," however, and had a wide network of friends. And he displayed considerable social acumen. Someone once pointed out that he could "lead out a young lady on the floor with the ease and elegance of a French dancing master."[15] He also had a quick wit. According to one story, a medical colleague with whom he had disagreed walked directly into his path on the street one day. The man said he didn't propose to step aside for a fool. Drake said he would, and moved out of the way.[16]

Drake named his literary group the Buckeye Club after his home, which he called Buckeye Hall.[17] He was immensely fond of the buckeye tree because one of his earliest Ohio memories was of a cabin made of buckeye on one of the tributaries of the Licking River. Although not a Buckeye by birth, he considered himself a "Buckeye by engrafting, or rather by inoculation," having drawn his early nourishment from a bowl made from buckeye wood. When he was toasted at the celebration of the forty-fifth anniversary of the settlement of Cincinnati in 1833, he took the opportunity to reiterate an earlier proposal that the buckeye be named Ohio's emblem.[18] The buckeye tree became and remains the official state tree, and although Drake doesn't always get credit for it, he probably should. Certainly he promoted the cause with regularity and grace. According to travel writer Harriet Martineau, who visited Cincinnati in 1835 and attended a meeting of the Buckeye Club at Drake's home, the accoutrements included a large buckeye bowl of lemonade, a ladle made of buckeye, "and symbolical sprigs of the same" decorating the walls.[19]

The Buckeye Club did not meet as regularly as the Semi-Colon Club, was not as large, and did not have as structured a format. According to one attendee, Edward Mansfield, it was small enough to fit into the parlor. However, the gatherings were highly cultured, with engaging conversation that never degenerated into gossip.[20] Mansfield said the group assembled about 7:30 p.m., and Drake rang a little bell for attention. Sometimes compositions were read, and other times there was a general discussion on a particular question, which may or may not have been announced in advance. Occasionally a poem or story was included. "There, in that little circle of ladies and gentlemen," Mansfield said, "I have heard many of the questions which have since occupied the public mind, talked over with an ability and a fullness of information which is seldom possessed by larger and more authoritative bodies."[21]

Many of the members of the Semi-Colon Club, including the Beecher women, also participated in the Buckeye Club, which continued until 1839, when Drake's daughters married. Drake then left for Louisville, where he lived off and on for the rest of his life.[22] However, he was buried in Cincinnati's Spring Grove Cemetery, and Cincinnati has named both a park and a medical rehabilitation hospital for him.

A fourth organization that was organized a little later, the Literary Club of Cincinnati, remains in existence today. We will cover it in due course. Unfortunately, insufficient information is available to include a chapter on an organization founded by black educator Peter H. Clark in 1869. It is said to have encouraged the study of literature and remained in existence until Clark left the city in the late nineteenth century.[23]

CHAPTER THREE

THE LITTLE WOMAN WHO WROTE THE BOOK

The story of Cincinnati's most famous author begins in 1832, when the trustees of Lane Theological Seminary recruited one of the country's preeminent preachers to run their Presbyterian school in Walnut Hills. The Reverend Lyman Beecher gathered his second wife, Harriet Porter; his unmarried stepsister, Esther; and six of his thirteen children (two others joined them later) in Boston and set out on a trek, via Philadelphia and New York, to the Queen City. Among those making the trip was Lyman's twenty-one-year-old daughter Harriet, who was to become one of America's most important literary figures.

Harriet Beecher Stowe, the woman Abraham Lincoln famously described in 1862 as the "little woman who wrote the book that started this Great War," lived in Cincinnati for almost eighteen years, and there she married, conceived her seven children, and buried the one she considered her favorite. She also published her first book in Cincinnati, honed her writing skills with the Semi-Colons, and met the man who launched her blockbuster, *Uncle Tom's Cabin*. Most importantly, it was in the river city of Cincinnati, where the free state of Ohio met the slave state of Kentucky, that she gathered the experiences and perspective for her influential book.

When the Beechers arrived in Cincinnati, after traveling by stagecoach to what is now Wheeling, West Virginia, and from there by boat, the city was on the upswing. It was growing so fast that in two decades it would become one of the country's largest cities. Its manufacturing and slaughterhouses were booming, and the city was a transportation hub, linking all parts of the country via the Ohio and Mississippi Rivers. The public landing was one of the busiest anywhere. Of course, as previously mentioned, the city was not merely "Porkopolis," with the rough-and-tumble persona the nickname implied; it was a place where culture was beginning to flourish. The educated and intellectual Beecher family was an important addition, on its way to becoming one of the foremost American families of the day. Lyman's children, in addition to Harriet, included Henry Ward, who would become a well-known minister, lecturer, and abolitionist; Catharine, an educator and writer who would found several schools for young women; and Isabella, who would become active in the women's suffrage movement.

The Beechers stayed in rented quarters downtown while Lyman's new house was built near the Lane campus on Gilbert Avenue.[1] They had relatives in the city and immediately felt at home. Roxanna Foote Beecher, Lyman's first wife and Harriet's mother, had two brothers who were city residents. John Parsons Foote, a type founder believed to be the city's first bookseller, had lived in the city since 1820. Samuel Foote, a sea captain and businessman who made a fortune after he arrived in 1828, built the mansion at Third and Vine where the Semi-Colons often met. The Foote brothers founded the Greater Cincinnati Water Works and were among the city's elite. Still another Cincinnati relation was the wealthy Edward King, a cousin of Harriet Porter's.[2]

In late 1833, the Beecher family moved into a new house at what is now 2950 Gilbert Avenue, about three miles north of downtown. The two-story brick building with a long L extending from the back originally had only four rooms: two on the first floor and two on the second. The grounds were filled with flowers, chickens, and a vegetable garden.[3] According to an unpublished paper written in 1949 for the Literary Club of Cincinnati, the property was so rural

FIGURE 3.1 Harriet Beecher Stowe House, 2950 Gilbert Avenue, Cincinnati. *Photograph by author*

that Lyman fished and gathered wild grapes and nuts in the woods nearby. He also kept a loaded shotgun or two in his study. When wild pigeons flocked overhead, he went out to the grove of beech trees behind his house and shot dinner.[4]

The Beechers thought their new neighborhood beautiful. "How I wish you could see Walnut Hills," Harriet wrote a friend. "It is about two miles from the city, and the road to it is as picturesque as you can imagine a road to be without 'springs that run among the hills.' Every possible variety of hill and vale of beautiful slope, and undulations of land set off by velvet richness of turf and broken up by groves and forests of every outline of foliage, make the scene Arcadian. You might ride over the same road a dozen times a day untired, for the constant variation of view caused by ascending and descending hills relieves you from all tedium."[5]

The industrious easterners didn't wait for their new house to be finished to get down to work. Lyman immediately assumed his duties as president of Lane Seminary and a few months later took a second job as pastor of Second Presbyterian Church, which was located downtown on Fourth Street between Vine and Race. (McAlpin's department store moved to the site in 1878.[6]) Sons Henry Ward and Charles enrolled as students at Lane, and George accepted a pastorate in nearby Batavia. (After several years of preaching, George took a break to study at Lane too.[7]) Catharine opened the Western Female Institute, a boarding school for girls, in a rented building downtown. Harriet joined her as associate principal and teacher,[8] and Isabella became a student at the school, boarding downtown during the week.[9]

In addition to teaching and helping to run the school, Harriet completed a textbook, *Primary Geography for Children*, that she had started before moving west. It was published in 1833 by a Cincinnati publisher, Corey and Fairbank. Catharine was listed as coauthor of the book, probably because of her reputation in the field of education, but the work is considered to be Harriet's. The bishop of Cincinnati praised the book for its unbiased image of Catholicism, and it proved both popular and lucrative. It was the first of some thirty books Stowe would publish in her lifetime.[10]

With so many influential relatives in town, as well as friends from the East, the Beecher family was immediately launched into the most exclusive social circles. Harriet and Catharine joined the Buckeye and Semi-Colon Clubs. Harriet perfected her writing skills for the Semi-Colon Club, and some biographers have suggested it may have been the single most important influence on her development as a writer.[11] She considered it so influential that she acknowledged it in the 1855 edition of her book *The Mayflower*, which included many of the pieces she wrote for the meetings. "There are those now scattered through the world," she said, "who will remember the social literary parties of Cincinnati, for whose genial meetings many of these articles were prepared. With most affectionate remembrances, the author dedicates the book to the yet surviving members of The Semicolon."[12]

But *The Mayflower* was not Harriet's first publication to draw on her Semi-Colon oeuvre. One piece, a character sketch of a man named Uncle Lot, was so good that fellow Semi-Colon member James Hall tracked down the unidentified author and convinced her to enter it in a contest for the *Western Monthly Magazine,* which he edited. The story won top prize and was published in April 1834 under the title "A New England Sketch." She received fifty dollars.[13]

In addition to their role in Harriet's writing career, the Semi-Colon soirees were important because they were where the young Harriet socialized with Eliza Stowe and her husband, Calvin, Lane professor of biblical literature. Eliza became a special friend of Harriet's, and after she died of cholera in 1834, Harriet and Calvin grew close as they comforted each other. They were married on January 6, 1836, in a quiet ceremony at her father's house on Gilbert Avenue. Two days later they took a "wedding excursion" to Columbus, Ohio, where Calvin had business.[14]

The Stowes' first residence was a small brick building where they awaited better faculty housing from Lane. When their new house came through, it was at 2622 Gilbert, on the site where the Church of the Assumption now stands, at the opposite side of the Lane campus from Lyman's house.[15] According to an 1896 newspaper article, the Stowes' was "a modest little home, at which no passer would glance a second time." Nevertheless, it was a pleasant place for Lane students to visit. Calvin and Harriet had an agreement: "When one should become moody and out of sorts the other should be cheerful enough to make up the deficiency."[16] However, Calvin spent long periods out of town, raising funds and buying books for Lane and doing research on European school systems. Harriet stopped teaching after she married and often moved back home with her father while Calvin was away. Her first children, twin girls, were born in Lyman's house.

Harriet's married life in Cincinnati included much happiness. In her later years, she remembered her time in Walnut Hills as the "Indian Summer" of her life, focused on her marriage and her family.[17] Six of her seven children were born in the city, and she was pregnant with the seventh when she moved away in 1850. And the Cincinnati years included much of her professional growth as well. Along with the activities of the Semi-Colon and Buckeye Clubs, she engaged in passionate intellectual discussion at the Beecher dinner table, avid letter writing with out-of-town friends and family, and the development of her literary career. In addition to *Primary Geography for Children, The Mayflower,* and her sketch in the *Western Monthly Magazine,* she published articles in the *Cincinnati Journal,* the *New-York Evangelist,* and *Godey's Lady's Book.* She probably published pieces in the *Cincinnati Chronicle* as well.[18]

Beginning in Cincinnati during the early years of her marriage, Harriet received support from Calvin for her literary interests. Her husband famously encouraged her to be a "literary woman" and suggested the rather unconventional idea that she write under the name "Harriet Beecher Stowe" rather than the more customary (and cumbersome) "Mrs. H. E. Beecher Stowe."[19]

But the Cincinnati years were hardly idyllic. The family had recurrent financial struggles, and Harriet was reduced to taking in boarders at one point. She also experienced an attack of cholera, a rapid succession of pregnancies, trying attempts to balance household management with a literary career, and several deaths, including her brother George's suicide in Chillicothe. And the family went through a number of significant controversies as well. For example, Lyman offended the city's large Catholic population soon after his arrival by implying that the western infidels needed missionaries to save them from eternal damnation.[20] Dr. Joshua L. Wilson, pastor of First Presbyterian Church, became a powerful enemy, which resulted in heresy charges being brought against Lyman. He was acquitted, but the episode was disturbing.[21]

More significant to Harriet's writing career was a major controversy that arose at Lane. One of the students Lyman had recruited, Theodore Dwight Weld, became class president and led rousing, influential, and now-famous discussions over abolition versus emancipation or colonization of slaves. During the Lane Debates, as they came to be known, the students fraternized with local African Americans, something Southern-leaning Cincinnatians could not tolerate. In 1834, while Lyman was raising funds elsewhere, the situation erupted. Lane's executive committee abolished the student organization and passed regulations limiting student activities. Most of the students walked out of the school, and though Lyman tried to stabilize things when he returned, his weak leadership and equivocal point of view, originally favoring colonization over abolition, proved disastrous. Many of the students ultimately moved to Oberlin College, and Lane never fully recovered.[22]

In April 1837, another pivotal event occurred. Abolitionist editor James G. Birney began publishing his antislavery newspaper, the *Philanthropist*, at A. H. Pugh Printing Company on Main Street. On July 12, a mob attacked his office and damaged the printing press, threatening further action if publication didn't cease. When the Ohio Anti-Slavery Society, sponsor of the *Philanthropist*, refused to suspend publication, Birney's office was attacked again. That time the publisher's press was hauled down to the river and destroyed. Harriet was in the thick of things and wrote a letter to the *Cincinnati Journal* about the dangers of condoning mob violence. (She was appalled that her Uncle John was among those who tried to suppress Birney.[23])

In addition to being extremely close to both the *Philanthropist* debacle and the Lane situation, Harriet was exposed to the issues of slavery in other ways. For example, she became acquainted with the Reverend John Rankin, who operated a station on the

Underground Railroad in Ripley, Ohio. Rankin had three sons enrolled at Lane, and Harriet and her father were his houseguests
while attending a church meeting in Ripley, about fifty miles east
of the city. It was from Rankin that Harriet heard the story of the
slave woman who escaped across the river on the ice, the real-life
model for the memorable Eliza in *Uncle Tom's Cabin*.[24]

Harriet gained additional experience with the Underground
Railroad when one of Rankin's sons became ill at Lane and asked
Calvin to transport a runaway slave to the next stop.[25] Harriet was
also on hand when Calvin and her brother Henry Ward Beecher
came to the aid of one of the Stowe servants. Her former master
was searching for her, despite the fact that she was then living in
a free state. Stowe and Beecher secreted the woman to John Van
Zandt's cabin in Glendale, some twelve miles away.[26]

Another influential experience for Harriet occurred on a visit to
Maysville, Kentucky, when she witnessed a slave auction in front of
the county courthouse in nearby Washington.[27]

Stowe was also moved in Cincinnati by stories of children being
ripped from slave mothers and given to others, by accounts of slave
women murdering their own children to avoid separation, and by
activities of Quaker friends who later became models for her Underground Railroad characters. She herself raised money to help a slave
woman whose three-year-old child was to be sold away from her.[28]

Another Cincinnati event critical to her empathetic view of the
slave situation was the July 1849 death of her sixth child, Samuel
Charles. Charley, as he was known, died of cholera at the age of
eighteen months, and Harriet was devastated. Later she wrote, "It
was at *his* dying bed, and at *his* grave that I learnt what a poor slave
mother may feel when her child is torn away from her."

In the spring of 1850, Calvin Stowe accepted a job at his alma
mater, Bowdoin College, and Harriet, six months pregnant with her
seventh child, went ahead to settle in Brunswick, Maine, while her
husband finished his teaching assignment at Lane. By the following

March she had delivered her baby and made the decision to write about slavery. She offered her story to an old friend from Cincinnati, Dr. Gamaliel Bailey Jr., a physician who had taught at Lane and worked on the *Philanthropist*. By then Bailey was editor of the *National Era* in Washington, and he gladly accepted her piece, entitled *Uncle Tom's Cabin; or, Life among the Lowly*, for serialization. The first installment appeared June 5, 1851, to momentous acclaim, and, when the complete story was published in book form in 1852, it sold ten thousand copies the first week.[29] Eventually translated into more than seventy-five languages, it has sold millions of copies and has never gone out of print. For part of the twentieth century the book and its main characters fell out of favor, but today their power and significance are well respected. *Uncle Tom's Cabin* is still used as a school text.

The Stowes moved to Andover, Massachusetts, in 1853 for Calvin to teach at Andover Theological Seminary. When he retired in 1864, they moved to Hartford, Connecticut, where they both continued writing at Nook Farm and eventually moved into a retirement cottage next door to the home of Mark Twain. Calvin died in 1886, and Harriet died ten years later.

It appears that Mrs. Stowe returned to Cincinnati only once, to fulfill a speaking engagement for the Mercantile Library in 1873.[30] According to a much later newspaper account, she visited her old home in Walnut Hills.[31] It seems likely that she would also have visited Charley's grave, which is believed to have been near her former home (it has since disappeared[32]).

Few tangible traces of the Beechers and the Stowes remain in Cincinnati. The most visible is Lyman Beecher's brick home, where Harriet often stayed. Known as the Harriet Beecher Stowe House, it is owned by the Ohio Historical Society and is open to the public. Lane Theological Seminary is gone, but a plaque on Gilbert Avenue near Thomson MacConnell Cadillac marks the site. The tower of a church with links to the school stands nearby. You can also see a bust of Harriet's Uncle John Foote, as well as a 2003 bust of Harriet herself, at the Mercantile Library.

Cincinnati's illustrious Spring Grove Cemetery holds the graves of John Foote and his wife, marked with simple rectangular stones. Harriet Porter Beecher and Eliza Stowe are there too, but their bodies were moved to Spring Grove from Walnut Hills in the late nineteenth century and lie in unmarked graves in a grassy open area. The school where Harriet and Catharine taught was torn down years ago, as was the Second Presbyterian Church, where Lyman preached.

CHAPTER FOUR

LEASES, LECTURES, AND A LIBRARY

On April 18, 1835, forty-five young merchants and clerks, people of humble beginnings and limited means, gathered on the second floor of a Cincinnati firehouse to form an organization to buy books. There were no public libraries at the time, and books were so expensive that they were available only to the rich, so the men pooled their resources. The organization they formed was among hundreds of such "membership libraries" established in the nineteenth century. Cincinnati's is one of only about twenty that remain, and is the oldest continuously operating library west of Philadelphia. In 2010, it celebrated its 175th anniversary.[1]

What was originally the Young Men's Mercantile Library Association, now the Mercantile Library of Cincinnati, is located at 414 Walnut Street on a site it has occupied since 1840. Rare marble busts, maple hardwood floors, and nine-foot stacks with a collection of approximately seventy-eight thousand books, some dating from the nineteenth century or earlier, grace the library, and a full-sized Grecian statue of Silence, finger to lips, warns that members might be reading (or snoozing!) in deep leather chairs. Demilune-capped double-hung windows throw patches of dusty sunlight onto slant-top reading desks. In 2009, the Mercantile was refurbished with fresh paint, a new mezzanine, and carefully concealed computer wires, but you can still relax in Stickley-style chairs, examine two-hundred-year-old books from glass-fronted cabinets, or simply read a newspaper in the ambience of a bygone day.[2]

FIGURE 4.1 The Mercantile Library reading room after 2010 refurbishment. *Courtesy of the Mercantile Library of Cincinnati*

The library's original building, now referred to as Old College Hall, burned down in January 1845, and, when college leaders struggled to rebuild, the library agreed to give them a desperately needed ten thousand dollars for a ten-thousand-year lease, renewable in perpetuity. The replacement building, New College Hall, was partially destroyed by fire in 1869 but was succeeded by the Cincinnati College Building that same year. That building gave way to the existing Mercantile Building in 1904, but, because of the airtight lease, credited to Alphonso Taft, father of U.S. president William Howard Taft, the library continues to reside on the site. The organization still functions as a membership library and is open to anyone for a small annual fee.[3]

Although the founders' original interest was books, and some of the first books they acquired remain in the collection today, it was not long before they envisioned another way to educate themselves in the frontier city that was then Cincinnati. During the library's first winter, they established the region's first lecture series. Joseph S. Benham, a prominent local attorney and professor of law who had been the orator for the marquis de Lafayette's visit to the city in 1825, was given the princely sum of two hundred dollars for lectures on commercial and mercantile law.[4]

A large man with a thundering voice and piercing eyes, Benham got the library off to a formidable beginning, but it was only the beginning. Although the library's records are incomplete, more than three hundred and fifty lectures during the first hundred years alone have been identified. Until the 1860s, when the Civil War affected the library's fortunes, the organization typically held long courses of lectures in the winter months. After the war, the remainder of the first hundred years is spotty, but there were several stellar lecture seasons and at least occasional attempts to revive the full winter course. There were also periods when members gave "practical papers" after business meetings; when classes were offered in French, German, mathematics, and other subjects; and when musical entertainments or dramatic readings were presented.

The Mercantile's list of lecturers is extraordinary. Among the most noteworthy during the first century of its existence were newspaperman Horace Greeley; scientist Louis Agassiz; educator Horace Mann; poet/essayist Oliver Wendell Holmes; orators Edward Everett and Henry Ward Beecher; and such accomplished writers as Ralph Waldo Emerson, William Makepeace Thackeray, Herman Melville, Bret Harte, and John Galsworthy. The list also includes some of the most prominent local citizens: Timothy Walker, Dr. Lyman Beecher, the astronomer Ormsby M. Mitchel, and Salmon P. Chase, the Ohio governor who became President Lincoln's treasury secretary and chief justice of the U.S. Supreme Court. Others were John W. Ellis, founder of First National Bank of Cincinnati (a forerunner of the mammoth U.S. Bank); William H. and

Alexander H. McGuffey, authors of McGuffey's *Readers;* and John Parsons Foote, Harriet Beecher Stowe's uncle.

Not as many lecturers were invited to the library in the fifty years after 1935, but Nobel Laureate Saul Bellow came to speak for the 150th anniversary in 1985, and since then there have been many. In 1987, inspired by the Bellow evening, community leaders Buck and Patti Niehoff established the annual Niehoff Lecture. It has featured such contemporary luminaries as Tom Wolfe, Jonathan Winters, Salman Rushdie, Margaret Truman, Calvin Trillin, David Baldacci, and Julia Child. And many authors have lectured there for other occasions, among them John Updike, E. L. Doctorow, Michael Cunningham, George Packer, and Samantha Power. A wide variety of discussion groups, debates, poetry readings, writers' workshops, and musical performances round out the library's year. And members continue to borrow books and use the reading room to read, browse magazines, work over brown-bag lunches, and relax in a quiet oasis away from their busy days.

Throughout its history, the library has made it a point to celebrate the anniversary of its founding. For example, the twenty-fifth anniversary, in 1860, an event billed as the quadri-centennial and planned with the assistance of a committee of 103 members, featured a grand evening for a large crowd. On April 18, evening had barely fallen when hacks and carriages "rattled over the pavements with twice their accustomed velocity, and wheeling in front of the beautiful temple [Pike's Opera House], and depositing their precious loads, would, like good Genii of fairy note, fly away again to repeat the act."[5] The featured lecturer of the evening was William Hooper, most likely the Cincinnati banker who donated funds to build the local Civil War battery, now home of the James A. Ramage Civil War Museum in Fort Wright, Kentucky. Hooper reflected at length on the history of libraries, on the Mercantile's influence on Cincinnati, and on the lecture program. He also rallied the guests to further improvements that would allow the library to compete "with the formidable competition of its most favored rival," the public library, which had been established in 1853. W. W. Fosdick presented a poem; noted actor and elocutionist James E. Murdoch gave dramatic readings; the living founders were honored; and Menter's Band, conducted by Mr. Menter himself, presented several selections.[6]

For the fiftieth anniversary, in 1885, there was a public program for library members and their friends at the Odeon. The stage was set in parlor style, with a variety of ornamental plants and flowers, and the program included selections by the Cincinnati Orchestra. Judge Samuel F. Hunt gave the anniversary address, contrasting the Cincinnati of the day with the Cincinnati of the founders and describing the library's rich history. Dr. A. C. Kemper read an original poem called "In the Library," and, as he had on many similar occasions, James E. Murdoch gave a recitation.[7]

Perhaps even more noteworthy from an historical perspective was the seventy-fifth anniversary celebration in 1910. For that event, U.S. president William Howard Taft was the speaker. Taft combined his visit to the Mercantile with a visit to the May Festival, arriving by train to major headlines. The Mercantile went all out, moving the newspaper racks and tables from the center of the reading room, adding a small speaker's platform in the southwest corner (where a permanent stage has recently been added), obtaining permission from the building's owner for the use of a second elevator, and securing donated plants from a local florist.[8]

On the morning of the noon event, the president of the library, prominent lawyer Charles B. Wilby, went to the residence of Charles Phelps Taft, the president's half brother, to escort the president to the library. "When a man comes home," Taft said in informal remarks, "he wants to go where he will feel most at home. I don't know any place which holds the memories of old Cincinnati to me more than the Mercantile Library." He then described his father's role in the library, which, in addition to lecturing, included the negotiation of the library's extraordinary ten-thousand-year, rent-free lease from the Law School College, then owner of the building. "There was a time when I was connected with the law school that I remember I thought the old gentleman was a bit too stiff in the matter of that lease," Taft said.

Taft pointed out that his father and his two brothers had been life members and that his own early reading had been "directed" at the library. And, he added, "The Mercantile Library has served many purposes beside the strictly library or literary." It has always been convenient, he said, for young men to meet their girls there, and the librarians "treasure many secrets it would never do to tell. I congratulate you. . . . My parting wish is God Bless the Mercantile Library."[9]

For the centenary celebration in 1935, the library started several months early. Leading up to the main event were four talks and teas featuring Cincinnati artist Dixie Selden, writer and University of Cincinnati dean Dr. Frank Wadleigh Chandler, prominent journalist and political commentator Dorothy Thompson (Mrs. Sinclair Lewis), and Miss Helen Hinkle, a frequent Cincinnati lecturer, who spoke on "The Story of the English Churchyard." For the actual anniversary in April, there was an open house at the library from 10 a.m. to 4 p.m., followed by a 7 p.m. birthday dinner in the spacious Marie Antoinette ballroom of the Hotel Alms, an elegant Cincinnati hotel that was decorated for the occasion with daffodils and other spring flowers. Some 245 guests were greeted by the librarian and the hospitality committee and seated at tables for ten. The four young literary figures who were invited to speak sat at a special table along the west side of the room: Herbert S. Agar, winner of the Pulitzer Prize in history for *The People's Choice;* Andrew Nelson Lytle, a founder of the Southern Agrarian Movement; noted poet, writer, and fellow Agrarian Allen Tate; and Seward Bishop Collins, editor of the *American Review* and the *Bookman.*[10]

For the 175th anniversary in 2010, the library opened the refurbished reading room and a new digital catalogue, raised money for construction and other projects, and presented an exceptional list of speakers, including humorist and journalist Bill Bryson for the Niehoff Lecture. They also held a party dubbed "A Big Noise at the Library" to celebrate the anniversary itself. A new history of the library and an anniversary poem were written by Dr. Robert C. Vitz and Dr. Norman Finkelstein, respectively.

At its highest point, in the nineteenth century, Mercantile membership exceeded four thousand.[11] By 1968, membership had dipped to less than three hundred, and the library rented out some of its space. In the late twentieth century, however, special events, membership parties, travel programs, and marketing efforts were undertaken, and, by 2000, membership had climbed to almost one thousand. With the increase in public interest, the library was able to reclaim its rented space and renovated it for use as a lecture and discussion hall. The elevator lobby to the reading room was also renovated, and a strategic planning process launched in 2003 led to a wide variety of other invigorated efforts. By 2009, membership had grown to about two thousand.

CHAPTER FIVE

READERS AND PUBLISHERS

"**M**cGuffey" is a name that appears frequently in Cincinnati histories, but what does it have to do with Cincinnati? A good question, given that William Holmes McGuffey, "schoolmaster to the nation," was not born in the Queen City, did not die there, and did not conceive his famous *Readers* there. In truth, claim to the McGuffey name might more properly belong to his home in Oxford, Ohio; at the log "schoolhouse" from his birth home at Detroit's Greenfield Village; or at the University of Virginia in Charlottesville, where he taught for many years, died, and was buried.

Yet Cincinnati can, indeed, claim a significant place in McGuffey's life, as well as in the making of his famous *Readers,* which sold an estimated one hundred and twenty million copies from 1836 to 1920 and another two hundred thousand during a revival in the 1980s.[1] The *Readers* promoted such values as honesty, thrift, hard work, and the Golden Rule and were considered as influential as the Bible or Webster's Dictionary. Cincinnati Public Schools used them as textbooks for twenty-five years, and they were popular throughout much of the United States, especially west of the Alleghenies and south of the Mason-Dixon Line. In the first half of the twentieth century, thousands of people tried to keep McGuffey values alive with McGuffey Societies.[2]

The story of the *Readers* begins with a Cincinnati printer in 1836. At that time, Cincinnati was the capital of western publishing,

FIGURE 5.1 William Holmes McGuffey. *Courtesy of the McGuffey Museum, Oxford, Ohio*

and Truman and Smith, a firm located on the second floor of a Main Street building between Fourth and Fifth Streets, was seeking a writer to craft a set of "eclectic" readers to complement a new arithmetic book. That book drew from a wide variety of literary and philosophical sources in what was then considered an avant-garde approach. Truman and Smith wanted to launch a similarly eclectic educational series. Their first choice for a writer was Catharine Beecher, Harriet Beecher Stowe's sister, who had only recently arrived in Cincinnati and had already established the Western Female Institute. She was a logical choice because she was deeply interested in the subject and had published several books on it, but she declined, preferring to focus on higher education. Whether she recommended William Holmes McGuffey, as some have suggested, or another member of her family proposed him, as others say, it was McGuffey who was then asked to take on the project.

McGuffey was a vibrant thirty-five-year-old professor of ancient languages at Miami University in Oxford, Ohio. Active in a variety of educational endeavors, he had already started working on a series of readers of his own.[3] In 1836, he signed a contract with Truman and Smith and produced the *First Reader* at the red brick Federal-style house on Spring Street in Oxford where he lived. That building, now the William Holmes McGuffey Museum and a National Historic Landmark, houses a rich repository of McGuffey materials, as well as his octagonal cherry desk, which he spun around to access the materials he needed to compile his stories and lessons.[4]

Even before his first book drew attention or he had delivered the second of the four books in his contract, McGuffey was recruited by Cincinnati's Daniel Drake and others to become president and professor of moral and intellectual philosophy at the newly organized Cincinnati College.[5] In the fall of 1836, he rented a house on Western Row, now Central Avenue, and moved his family to the city.[6] Unfortunately, the financial panic of 1837 soon hit, and the school was forced to close after three years, putting McGuffey out of a job. Nevertheless, he continued writing, and by 1837 he had fulfilled his contract.[7]

McGuffey was part of a select crowd in Cincinnati that included the Beechers, the Stowes, the Drakes, Edward D. Mansfield, and other intellectuals. After Calvin Stowe went to Europe in 1837 to study educational systems, McGuffey was among those who lobbied with him to organize Ohio's common schools. He and his friends also participated in an organization called the College of Teachers, later the Western Literary Institute, which presented lectures and promoted various literary and educational causes. It was material from the College of Teachers that formed the basis of McGuffey's *Fourth Reader*.[8]

McGuffey's books were gaining popularity in 1839, but, since they were only a sideline for him, he needed work. Drake recommended him as president of Ohio University in Athens, but the job did not go well. During his four years there, McGuffey became entangled in a fierce fight with the community over a now-famous grove of elm trees that he planted and fenced in on campus, eliminating locals' grazing rights. The townspeople pelted him with mud balls and burned him in effigy. By 1843, he was so unhappy he packed up and moved back to Cincinnati, where he got a job as president of what was then Woodward College.[9] He and his family moved in with his brother, Alexander Hamilton McGuffey, a lawyer sixteen years his junior, who lived in a two-and-a-half-story home called "Sunbright," at the foot of Southern Avenue in Mount Auburn. (Sunbright was remodeled into an apartment building in 1925, but the property is now vacant.[10]) With William's blessing, Alexander was commissioned to write the *Rhetorical Guide*, which later became the *Fifth Reader*, and the *Eclectic Speller*. He also worked on the *Sixth Reader*.[11]

By all accounts, Alexander was a brilliant man. He taught school at Woodward while working on a law degree, and, in 1839, after graduation from the Cincinnati College of Law, he opened a law office. He spent most of his career practicing law in the city and was a prominent civic leader: director of McMicken University (later the University of Cincinnati), secretary/treasurer of Cincinnati College, and president of the board of trustees at Miami Medical School. After the death of his first wife, Daniel Drake's daughter Elizabeth, he married Caroline Virginia Rich of Boston, who became a well-known hostess. She entertained such prominent local families as the Hickenloopers, Groesbecks, Emerys, and Tafts, as well as the English historian Edward A. Freeman and P. T. Barnum's General Tom Thumb, Charles Stratton.[12]

After several years, William McGuffey left Cincinnati again, this time for the University of Virginia, where he found a permanent home as professor of moral philosophy and political economy. He taught there for twenty-eight years and died on May 4, 1873, at the age of seventy-two.[13]

Those facts form the bare outline of the story, but they fail to reflect the most important Cincinnati connection and certainly don't reveal the most interesting twists and turns of history. For those, we must look to the publishing side of the story, for the McGuffey series not only began with a commissioned work by a Cincinnati firm, it also succeeded largely because of the efforts of a single Cincinnati printer. Detailed published histories show that Winthrop B. Smith was a man already experienced in the book business when he came to Cincinnati and went into partnership with W. T. Truman in 1833. He saw a future in textbook publishing and pursued it, while Truman developed other lines of business. The two didn't get along well, so in 1843 the partnership was dissolved. According to a popular story, Smith arrived at their office on Main Street early one day and made two piles of the books they had published. The smaller pile was composed of textbooks, the larger of other types of books. On top of the latter Smith stacked all the company's cash. When Truman arrived, Smith announced that he wanted to close the firm and asked his partner to pick the pile of his choice. Of course, Truman chose the large pile with the cash. And thus, according to the story, shrewd Cincinnati businessman

Winthrop B. Smith became sole owner of the now famous and ultimately highly profitable McGuffey *Readers.*

That story may be apocryphal, but probably isn't far from the truth, because a legal document still in existence shows that, for the meager sum of five hundred dollars, Smith acquired the rights to the firm's textbooks in 1843. The legal document may simply have confirmed a handshake deal. Regardless, Smith was an astute businessman. For example, it was he, and not McGuffey, who chose the popular word "eclectic" to include in the title—a clever marketing strategy that sold books.[14]

But Smith's marketing skill is evident in other ways. He was the one who handled promotion, saw to the editing of the books, sent the author, after the Civil War, on what today would be called a book tour, and managed to keep the McGuffey name legitimately connected to the project long after either McGuffey or his brother spent any significant time on it.

In 1838, when a plagiarism suit was brought against McGuffey, it was Smith who figured out what to do. It was common practice in those days for authors to "borrow" sections from other books, and indeed Smith expected McGuffey to do just that: he provided him with some seventy competitive readers for the purpose. Nevertheless, a lawsuit ensued, possibly, as some have suggested, because other publishers were concerned about the growing popularity of the *Readers.* Catharine Beecher and others came to McGuffey's defense in print, but Smith did something more practical. While the lawsuit was pending, he rushed out a reprint of the offending edition, substituting fresh material for any item that could possibly be questioned. By the time the suit came to court, he and McGuffey could truthfully argue that the problematic volume was no longer in print. They settled the case for two thousand dollars, a fraction of what had been demanded.[15]

Smith also neatly dealt with difficulties that arose during the Civil War. For example, when his shipment of books to secession states was cut off by embargoes, he made a duplicate set of plates and sent them to Nashville so that the printing could be done there by friends. The ingenious solution kept the McGuffey presence alive during the war.[16]

Smith developed another feature of the *Readers* that was to become important. The first editions included what would now be called stock art, but soon he commissioned original illustrations that were both realistic and compelling for young readers. Several of the most important illustrators of the nineteenth century, including Henry Farny, got their start drawing for McGuffey books.

Smith also hired staff editors who contributed significantly to the *Readers'* success. Two of the most notable were Cincinnati residents Timothy Stone Pinneo and Obed J. Wilson.

Smith was shrewd not only when he cut the financial deal with his partner but in his dealings with the McGuffeys. William was paid royalties of only 10 percent, up to a grand total of one thousand dollars, for his work on the first four *Readers*. After that, all rights reverted to Truman and Smith. The publisher did pay travel and lecture fees, a fee for writing a primer (which proved highly lucrative), and, in later years, a small annuity for approving revisions and for the use of the McGuffey name. And McGuffey received a barrel of choice smoked hams at Christmas. But all the various payments added up to a relatively small sum for such successful books. What they really did was tie McGuffey to the work throughout his lifetime, keeping the popular McGuffey brand alive.

Some people thought McGuffey was swindled by his publishers, but he apparently never thought so. An ordained Presbyterian minister, he considered preaching, teaching, and lecturing his real work. He believed the publishers were the ones who had made his books successful and that they deserved the financial rewards. He was probably right.[17]

Although Alexander McGuffey was paid small sums for his writing and was actually hired as in-house legal counsel by the publisher at one point, he and his descendants were less pleased with how the relationship evolved. One descendant quipped that ten Cincinnatians became millionaires from the *Readers*, but none of them were McGuffeys.

Alexander himself came to consider his writing for the *Readers* "hackwork" and grew displeased with some of the editing that was done.[18] According to one story, he had his name removed from the books after the publisher started using "A. H. McGuffey" in a flowery script that invited confusion with "W. H. McGuffey." The publishers are said to have quietly let it be assumed that William wrote those books too.

Many editions of the McGuffey *Readers* were published, and extensive editing was done, so some editions bear little resemblance to their original texts. One editor actually changed the names of the children in a book she was editing to those of her favorite nieces and nephews![19]

Smith's firm was reorganized a number of times and operated under several names, but Smith himself stayed involved until 1868, when he retired from the firm and moved away. If he hadn't become a millionaire in Cincinnati, he had certainly done well enough. He had built an Italianate villa with a tower and spacious verandas in the Clifton neighborhood, where he was considered one of the "barons" of Clifton. His successor in the printing firm, Obed J. Wilson, acquired the villa when Smith left town; it was torn down in the 1960s to make room for a housing development.[20]

In 1890, the firm then publishing the *Readers* merged with several other book companies to form the American Book Company, which became the largest publisher of textbooks in the country and one of the largest in the world. It continued publishing various editions of McGuffey *Readers* until the 1960s, but ceased to exist as an imprint after it was acquired by D. C. Heath and Company in 1981.[21] At the American Book Company Building, located on Pike Street at the south end of the Taft Museum in downtown Cincinnati, books were published from 1904 to 1972. Inside the

Renaissance Revival building, which now houses a company dealing in scrap metals, you can still pick up a brochure about the *Readers*, see framed reproductions from some of the McGuffey illustrations, and peruse a collection of the books behind the glass doors of a cabinet. On the frieze metopes are open books, with "AB" on one page and "Co" on the other. Between the letters is a torch symbolizing learning. The same logo appears on a tile mosaic on the floor between the double doors at the front entrance.[22]

FIGURE 5.2 American Book Company mosaic at the Renaissance Revival building on Pike Street. *Photograph by Louis E. Enzweiler*

CHAPTER SIX

A POEM IN THE PICTURE

Thomas Buchanan Read is not a name that many people know today, but there was a time when almost every schoolboy could recite by heart the clip-clop rhythms of his poem "Sheridan's Ride": "Up from the South, at break of day, / Bringing to Winchester fresh dismay." Read wrote and first presented the poem to the public in Cincinnati, but it was not the nineteenth-century poet/painter's only connection to the city. Although he spent long stretches of his colorful life in London, Paris, Rome, Boston, New York, Philadelphia, and Florence, he always returned to the Queen City.

The son of a poor family from Chester County, Pennsylvania, Read first came to Cincinnati in 1837 at the age of fifteen, crossing the Allegheny Mountains alone on foot and taking a flatboat down the Ohio River. He lived with a married sister and her husband, plow maker Cyrus Garrett, on Eighth Street, supporting himself with odd jobs—working in a grocery store, making cigars, painting signs, carving tombstones for the sculptor Shobal Vail Clevenger, and playing female roles for a Dayton theatrical company. Eventually, however, his fortunes changed. He persuaded wealthy arts patron Nicholas Longworth, a friend of Clevenger's, to finance a studio, and, with Longworth's help, won a commission to paint a portrait of General William Henry Harrison, then Whig candidate for president.[1] He also started writing poetry for local newspapers.[2] At eighteen, he was on his way.

Even though he was doing well, Read decided to move to New York in 1841, and a year later he left for Boston, where he socialized with such prominent literary figures as Henry Wadsworth Longfellow and Oliver Wendell Holmes. Some say Longfellow encouraged him to pursue poetry, but whether that is true or not, he did continue publishing. Later he painted portraits of Holmes, Longfellow, and Longfellow's three daughters.[3]

Read lived in Philadelphia for awhile, visited Europe, and published his first book of poetry, but the early 1850s found him back in Cincinnati, where he became a member of both the Sketch Club, an organization fostering art, and the Literary Club. For the Literary Club he wrote at least one paper and read it to the group.[4] He also spoke at the Mercantile Library. The Mercantile liked his work so much they chose him to write their anniversary poem for 1852. It was entitled "The Onward Age," and, according to one of his friends, he wrote the last lines as the carriage waited to take him to the hall to read it.[5]

Read spent the later part of the 1850s in Europe, where he continued painting and writing. In Italy, he hired the now-famous Cincinnati artist Henry Farny, who had done McGuffey illustrations, as a studio assistant. He also wrote a long poem about the American Revolution, *The Wagoner of the Alleghanies: A Poem of the Days of Seventy-Six.*[6]

When the Civil War broke out, he returned to Cincinnati, where he remained from 1861 to 1867. He moved in once again with his relatives on Eighth Street, and this time he set up a studio on Fourth Street.[7] The actor/elocutionist James E. Murdoch, who lived on a farm near Cincinnati, admired Read's *Wagoner* and thought parts of it would be a good addition to his performance repertoire. He gave the poem its first public reading at the Cincinnati Academy of Music for the benefit of sick and wounded soldiers. The results were "electrical," and he and Read started rehearsals for a national tour to raise money for the war effort.[8]

In late 1862, Read wrote another poem that became popular—
so popular, in fact, that President Abraham Lincoln requested it
during one of Murdoch's Washington performances. When Murdoch replied that he regretted he didn't have a copy with him,
Lincoln said, "Oh that is easily remedied: I have 'The Swear' in
my pocket."[9]

In 1862, Read became a Cincinnati war correspondent of sorts.
Confederate troops were moving north through Kentucky, and
Cincinnati feared an imminent attack. General Lew Wallace, later
the author of the novel *Ben-Hur: A Tale of the Christ,* took charge
of the defense, rushing the city into a frenzy of preparation. Wallace called for volunteer aides, and Read reported for duty. "Come
on!" Wallace shouted to the approximately 150 men who had gathered, and charged off in search of a fight. After a while he stopped
and looked back. "Of the whole array there were but two within
call," he recounted later. One was Read.

The Confederates withdrew in the end, and what Read dubbed
"the Siege of Cincinnati" was averted. Read reported the story for
the February 1863 issue of the *Atlantic Monthly.*

Shortly after the Cincinnati skirmishes, Read joined the Army
of the Cumberland in Tennessee, but that did not stop him from
pursuing poetry. He had a genial personality and often favored the
troops with recitations of his verse. On one occasion he entertained
future U.S. president General James A. Garfield. According to a
first-hand observer, his presentation was a bit too flowery for most
of the soldiers.[10]

Read's most celebrated war poem was written in the upstairs
bedroom of a three-story house in downtown Cincinnati, not at
the front.[11] On Monday, October 31, 1864, while Read was staying with his sister and Cyrus Garrett, Garrett brought home the
latest issue of *Harper's Weekly.* The cover featured a Thomas Nast
illustration of Union General Philip Henry Sheridan's "Ride to
the Front" on his black horse, Rienzi. Inside was an account of

Sheridan's October 19 ride from Winchester in the Shenandoah Valley to Cedar Creek, where he found his troops in retreat. Sheridan rallied his men, fended off another attack, and counterattacked. What had been a disaster was turned into a victory.

Garrett showed Read the illustration. "Buck," he said, "there is a poem in that picture." He went on to suggest to their friend Murdoch that perhaps Read could write something for a performance Murdoch was giving that evening at Pike's Opera House. Both men protested. "I shall not have time to look it over and catch its inner meaning and beauties, and besides I am not in the habit of reading a poem at night written in the morning," Murdoch said. "Do you suppose I can write a poem to order—just as you would go to Sprague's and order a coat?" Read said.

But Read decided to give it a try anyway. He left instructions not to be disturbed unless the house caught fire, and went upstairs to write. A few hours later he emerged with a seven-stanza poem. Murdoch presented it that evening at Pike's, and the crowd of several thousand people erupted in "rapturous applause."[12]

The *Cincinnati Commercial* asked for a copy of "Sheridan's Ride" immediately after the performance, but Read demurred, saying it was still in rough form. However, he made few, if any, changes, and a week later a friend, the poet Bayard Taylor, sent the poem to Horace Greeley's *New York Tribune*. The *Tribune* published it on the front page on election day 1864, and other newspapers around the country quickly followed suit.

"Sheridan's Ride" is regarded as having been influential in Lincoln's reelection to the presidency. At least it can be said to have captured the public imagination and quickly popularized Read's name. Unfortunately, popularity was about all he got out of it. He tried to capitalize on his success by sculpting a bust of Sheridan and painting several canvases of the ride scene, which he intended to use to produce lithographs, but the latter project was incomplete at his death. He never made much money.[13]

One project Read did complete, in 1865, was a portrait of Indiana governor Oliver P. Morton, which he undertook at the request of Cincinnati's City Council. Read was hired to paint the portrait in gratitude for Morton's assistance to the city during the siege of Cincinnati. A biographer of Morton's notes that Morton didn't care for it, but it is believed to have hung in the Cincinnati Council chambers for many years. (Recently the city's conservator was unable to locate the painting or provide information on its whereabouts.)

Morton's biographer also describes an evening when Morton, Read, Murdoch, and others gathered in a basement room of Cincinnati's Burnet House and caroused until 2 a.m. Murdoch delivered segments from Shakespeare's *Hamlet*, Read recited his own verses, and others provided jokes and tales. They all consumed a large quantity of Catawba wine.[14]

In 1867, Read returned to Europe, but not before commemorating another Cincinnati event. He wrote an occasional poem entitled "Pons Maximus" to mark the opening of a bridge, now known as the John A. Roebling Cincinnati Suspension Bridge, which spanned the Ohio River and connected Cincinnati and Covington, Kentucky. Although the poem does not appear in Read's collected works, and all efforts to locate a copy have been unsuccessful, it is said to have been one of his most popular poems.[15]

Read continued to write and paint when he returned to Rome, but he was involved in a carriage accident, and his health declined. On Sunday, March 10, 1872, some of his friends gathered in Cincinnati to toast his fiftieth birthday, which was two days away, and cabled him in Rome with birthday wishes. The telegram, which arrived while he was in the middle of a supper party, brought tears to his eyes. He quickly fired back a cable saying that he would respond to the greeting in person, and left for Cincinnati soon afterward. He never made it.[16] He developed pneumonia en route, and when he reached New York on the steamship *Scotia* he was

FIGURE 6.1   Eighth Street plaque marking where T. Buchanan Read wrote "Sheridan's Ride." *Photograph by Louis E. Enzweiler*

taken to the Astor House, where he died on May 11, 1872.[17] He was buried in Pennsylvania. The Sheridan, the house at what is now 21 East Eighth Street where he wrote his famous poem, has been torn down. A simple plaque marks the spot.[18]

CHAPTER SEVEN

THE POET SISTERS

F ronting on Hamilton Avenue in what is now North College Hill sits Cary Cottage, a charming two-story painted brick farmhouse that is the focal point of one of Cincinnati's most interesting literary stories. If not a rags-to-riches tale, it is at least a country-girl-to-bluestocking tale, and that isn't all: it includes a ghost story, the biographical beginnings of two of the country's earliest feminists, and Ohio's first home for blind women.

Cary Cottage did not foster any published work until the late 1830s, but stories related to the site go back to 1814, when Robert Cary and Elizabeth Jessup started their married life in a small frame house on a quarter share of family property in what was then Mount Pleasant, later Mount Healthy, about eight miles north of downtown Cincinnati. The Carys worked hard to pay for their farm, which they called Clovernook, and to support their growing family, which ultimately included nine children. After eighteen years, they were able to build their dream house, the three-bedroom brick cottage that remains on the tract today. The house was listed on the National Register of Historic Places in 1973 and has a widespread reputation as home of "the poet sisters," the couple's fourth and sixth children, Alice and Phoebe Cary. In their lifetimes, the Cary sisters developed a national reputation for their poetry, novels, and hymns, as well as for their brilliant New York literary salons. They also attracted the attention of such literary celebrities as Edgar Allan Poe, John Greenleaf Whittier, and Horace Greeley.[1]

FIGURE 7.1 Cary Cottage in North College Hill. *Photograph by author*

Long before the Carys developed literary reputations, however, they reported one of the few ghost stories associated with the Cincinnati area. According to Alice, who was twelve at the time, the sighting occurred in 1832, just as their new house was completed. "There had been a violent shower; father had come home from the field, and everybody had come in out of the rain. I think it was about four in the afternoon, when the storm ceased and the sun shone out," she said. "The new house stood on the edge of a ravine, and the sun was shining full upon it, when someone in the family called out and asked how [sisters] Rhoda and Lucy came to be over in the new house, and the door open." Everyone rushed to see, and there was Rhoda in the open doorway, with Lucy in her arms. They called to her, but she didn't answer. Then the real Rhoda, who had put Lucy to sleep in the upstairs bedroom, came down the steps near them. Rhoda stood with the family "while we all saw, in the full blaze of the sun, the woman with the child in her arms slowly sink, sink, sink into the ground, until she disappeared from sight." Silence and a great feeling of sorrow engulfed them. No one knew why.

The following fall, Rhoda and Lucy both succumbed to typhoid fever, dying within a month of one another.[2] The remaining family members believed that the ghosts they had seen had been a premonition, and from that time on they often spotted an apparition of Lucy, dressed in a favorite red dress, on the property. Ghostly sightings in and around the cottage have been reported in modern times by people unrelated to the family.

The deaths of the sisters deeply scarred the family and made an indelible impression on Alice in particular. Beyond that, however, life on the farm was just plain hard. Though the senior Carys liked to read, they placed limited value on education and owned fewer than a dozen books. Alice and Phoebe attended a nearby school for a few years, but the family focus was primarily on work at home. And, in 1835, they experienced another loss: their mother died. Their father remarried two years later, but the childless widow he chose did not get along well with the children. Her only interest was the daily chores, and she did not approve of the reading and studying the children wanted to do. Alice and Phoebe, who had begun writing poems when they were young, went underground, doing their writing after their father and stepmother retired for the evening and hiding their poems in a cupboard to avoid detection. They wrote by the light of a rag wick, set in a saucer of lard, because candles couldn't be "wasted."

In 1838, eighteen-year-old Alice's first poem, "The Child of Sorrow," appeared in a Cincinnati Universalist newspaper, the *Sentinel*.[3] That same year, fourteen-year-old Phoebe secretly sent a poem to a Boston newspaper and discovered that it had been accepted only after she came upon a reprint in a Cincinnati newspaper.

Family relations were so strained that Robert Cary built a new house on the property and moved there with his wife in 1839, leaving Alice and Phoebe to care for their three young siblings. The new arrangement meant additional work for the sisters, but they considered it a blessing. They were able to write more freely and published regularly for about ten years. Although they were not paid, their work often appeared in daily and weekly Cincinnati journals and Universalist Church publications. Among the most prominent were the Boston *Ladies' Repository,* the *Ladies' Repository* of Cincinnati, and *Graham's Magazine.*

In the late 1840s, family connections in Cincinnati finally sparked Alice's writing career. William D. Gallagher, a distant cousin and perhaps the city's best-known poet of the day, introduced the sisters to Gamaliel Bailey Jr., editor of the *Philanthropist* and later the *National Era,* which serialized Harriet Beecher Stowe's *Uncle Tom's Cabin.* Bailey began publishing Alice's poetry in the *National Era* and paid her ten dollars in 1847 for the first piece of her prose to be published. (It was written under the pen name Patty Lee.) About that time, the poet John Greenleaf Whittier, who happened to be a contributing editor of the *National Era,* reviewed a Cincinnati publication called *Herald of Truth* and took the opportunity to give Alice's work a positive mention. Alice wrote to thank him, and a lifelong friendship ensued.[4]

The next year, Rufus W. Griswold, a well-known editor and critic who had seen Alice's work in western newspapers, wrote to request a poem for his anthology *The Female Poets of America.* In a review in the *Southern Literary Messenger,* Edgar Allan Poe praised Alice's "Pictures of Memory" as "the noblest poem in the collection."[5] By 1850, the Carys had garnered such widespread attention that acclaimed newspaper editor Horace Greeley actually called on them at Cary Cottage. That year, Griswold made arrangements for the

FIGURE 7.2 Alice Cary, as shown in *A Memorial of Alice and Phoebe Cary* by Mary Clemmer Ames, 1873

sisters' first book, *Poems of Alice and Phoebe Carey* [*sic*], to be published by Moss and Brother of Philadelphia.

That same year, Alice and Phoebe did a little social calling themselves. In a daring trip for young single women of the day, they traveled to the Northeast to visit those who had expressed interest in their poetry. Among them was Whittier, who later commemorated the occasion in a poem entitled "The Singer," which began,

> Years since (but names to me before),
> Two sisters sought at eve my door;
> Two song-birds wandering from their nest,
> A gray old farm-house in the West.

After several months in the East, the women returned home, but Alice decided almost immediately to move to New York, where she planned to support herself with poetry. Phoebe and Elmina joined her after a while, and the three women lived frugally in rented rooms, meticulously creating a homelike atmosphere. They also began actively pursuing their publishing interests and entertaining their prominent friends, including Greeley.

Despite the move to New York, Cincinnati was far from out of the picture for Alice. She continued writing for Cincinnati's *Ladies' Repository,* to which she was still under contract. In New York, she also published her first fiction, *Hagar, a Story of To-Day,* in serialized installments for the *Cincinnati Commercial.* And she initiated the Clovernook books, collections of fictional sketches and essays based on her life in Ohio. They are now her best-known work.[6]

By 1856, Alice was successful enough to buy a house on New York's Twentieth Street, where she and her sisters could live in more comfortable surroundings. They created a large library that vastly overshadowed the single shelf of books their parents had owned. They also initiated Sunday salons, which they conducted weekly for fifteen years. These are sometimes considered upscale forerunners of the famous Greenwich Village writers' groups. Among the celebrities who attended were editor and social reformer Robert Dale Owen; poet and literary critic Bayard Taylor; women's rights leader Elizabeth Cady Stanton; author Mary Mapes Dodge (*Hans Brinker, or The Silver Skates*); and circus founder P. T. Barnum. Whittier and Greeley were frequent guests as well.

Both Alice and Phoebe were engaged in the early feminist movement, and Alice was asked to become the first chair of the New York Woman's Club, later known as Sorosis. For a short time, Phoebe, the more active feminist of the two, served as assistant editor of the *Revolution,* a newspaper published by women's rights leader Susan B. Anthony. One of Phoebe's most popular poems was "Was He Henpecked?"[7]

Phoebe managed the household for the sisters and spent less time writing than Alice did, but she was able to publish several books and developed a strong following. She is said to have been a wonderful conversationalist and is sometimes described as the wittiest woman in America at the time. She is best remembered for her parodies, religious verses, and hymns, including the popular "Nearer Home."[8]

Alice also enjoyed an enviable career as a magazine and newspaper writer, appearing in *Harper's Weekly,* the *Atlantic Monthly,* and other prestigious publications. Some of her books were sold in England, and some were translated into French. For a decade she published a poem a week in the *New York Ledger.* She became so well known that couples often named their daughters after her.

Alice Cary died on February 12, 1871, at the age of fifty, after a long illness. Her sister and lifelong companion Phoebe died six months later. Both, after being commemorated with large funerals that were well attended by their intellectual friends, were buried in Brooklyn's Greenwood Cemetery. Together they had published more than fifteen books of prose, poetry, essays, fiction, and social commentary, as well as countless individual poems, hymns, and sketches. Although they won the hearts of the people of their time, their works are seldom read or mentioned today, probably because they are a bit sentimental for modern tastes. However, some literary critics argue that their voices are still important, both because of the element of early realism they provided and because they offered strong feminine and regional voices at a time when such voices were new. At the very least, the Carys are an inspiring success story: two poor young farm girls who made a literary mark.

In 1903, William A. Procter, one of the founders of Cincinnati consumer goods firm Procter and Gamble, helped two other young women, Florence and her blind sister Georgia Trader, buy the Cary farm and establish Ohio's first home for blind women in Cary Cottage. The Clovernook Center for the Blind and Visually Impaired is still situated on the Cary land, though it has moved out of Cary Cottage. The small house where the Cary sisters wrote their earliest poems has been restored with period furnishings and opened to the public. Visitors find portraits of Alice and Phoebe, the cupboard where they hid their work, the fireplace where they cooked their meals, and a small ladder-back chair marked with Phoebe's initials. With luck, they may also be able to catch a glimpse of a little girl in a red dress.

CHAPTER EIGHT

THE FATHER OF THE QUEEN

M any Cincinnatians know that the city's famous nickname, "the Queen of the West," is somehow related to the poet Henry Wadsworth Longfellow, author of "Paul Revere's Ride" and "The Village Blacksmith." But why did Longfellow write about Cincinnati? Did he ever visit the city? What was the connection?

First the basics: in an 1850 poem titled "Catawba Wine," Longfellow praised the Catawba grape that won honors at the Ohio Mechanics Institute's annual fair: "To the Queen of the West, / In her garlands dressed, / On the banks of the Beautiful River," the poem reads. The full text of "Catawba Wine" can be found in the collection *Birds of Passage*, along with other Longfellow poems originally published in various periodicals. There you can find an inscription that yields an important clue to the poem's Cincinnati connection: "Written on the receipt of a gift of Catawba wine from the vineyards of Nicholas Longworth on the Ohio River."[1]

A full-length portrait of Nicholas Longworth hangs in the Taft Museum of Art, which was once Belmont, Longworth's home.[2] A somber-looking Longworth, dressed in a black suit, with a white shirt and a dark tie, has a reminder note of some sort pinned to his sleeve. Grape vines trail from a table near his left arm as he looks out from Belmont over the terraced vineyards of what is now the urban community of Mount Adams. Longworth has shaggy, unkempt eyebrows, one of which is cocked several degrees higher than the other, and his eyes are so sharp that in person he is said to have startled little

FIGURE 8.1 Portrait of Nicholas Longworth by Robert Duncanson, 1858. Oil on canvas. *Collection of the University of Cincinnati. Photograph courtesy of the Taft Museum of Art*

boys. But despite his colorful personality, gruff demeanor, rumpled clothes, and straightforward, strongly worded opinions, he was one of the country's richest men. He is recognized today as an important horticulturist and father of the American wine industry.

Nicholas Longworth came to Cincinnati from Newark, New Jersey, in 1803 and studied law with Judge Jacob Burnet, an associate justice of the Ohio Supreme Court and founder of the famous Burnet House hotel. Longworth soon gave up law for real estate and became the largest landowner in town. He also pursued a passion for botany and began experimenting with the cultivation of flowers, vegetables, and trees, introducing quite a few into popular usage. "You couldn't throw that man into the Ohio River," one man said, "without his coming to the surface, a rare species of fish in one hand, a fresh-water pearl in the other."[3]

Longworth liked to dress like a gardener while working on his estate. According to one story, a tall lawyer from Illinois named Abraham Lincoln came to Cincinnati to try a case and decided to visit the well-known grounds of Belmont. He mistook Longworth for the gardener and asked for a tour, which Longworth gladly gave. Only afterward did "Old Longworth," as he liked to call himself, disclose his true identity.[4]

One of Longworth's interests was making wine, both because he liked horticulture and because, as a believer in the temperance movement, he wanted to develop a mild wine that would replace the strong whiskey that was so popular. Around 1825, he became convinced that the Catawba grape was the variety he needed.[5]

Longworth's first Catawbas were mild, but they were not commercially successful until he began separating the skins from the juice before fermentation, a process that produced a wine similar to a white Zinfandel today. He expanded his experiments, and in 1842 there was a breakthrough. Some of the wine accidentally underwent a second fermentation, creating a new drink that, with the help of winemakers from Champagne, France, Longworth turned into a

FIGURE 8.2 Nicholas Longworth's home on Pike Street, now the Taft Museum of Art. *Photograph by author*

successful sparkling Catawba. By the mid-1850s, he was producing one hundred thousand bottles a year and turning a profit. After he died in 1863, his bottling plant was closed and purchased by a brewery, but by that time his claim as producer of America's first champagne was assured.[6] (Catawba wine is still made in New York.[7])

As it turns out, though, it wasn't Nicholas who made the initial contact with Longfellow, but his son. And it wasn't wine, but poetry, that sealed the friendship. In March 1840, Nicholas's twenty-seven-year-old son Joseph wrote admiringly of Longfellow's poetry in a letter to the Reverend and Mrs. Jared Sparks. Mrs. Sparks, whose husband later became president of Harvard University, forwarded the letter to Longfellow. "I am pleased to work thus on the hearts of the young," Longfellow wrote in a letter to his mother.[8] That was the beginning of a friendship between Longworth and Longfellow that lasted the rest of their lives and eventually encompassed

FIGURE 8.3 Henry Wadsworth Longfellow, plaster copy of Sir Thomas Brock's marble for Poets' Corner at Westminster Abbey. *Courtesy of the Mercantile Library of Cincinnati*

Joseph's famous father as well as other members of the Longworth and Longfellow families.

Joseph Longworth was a significant figure in his own right. Like his father, he was a major supporter of the arts and was instrumental in the founding of the Cincinnati Art Academy and the Cincinnati Art Museum. He also helped organize a still-prestigious private club, to which he affixed the name immortalized in Longfellow's poem: the Queen City Club. In 1845, he married into a prominent Southern family and built a two-story Italianate villa called Rookwood, named for a large population of crows, or rooks, which occupied the surrounding oak trees.[9] The home was situated on a one-hundred-acre tract on Grandin Road, where the Cincinnati Country Club now stands, and attracted such famous visitors as Thackeray and Emerson, probably while they were in town to speak under the auspices of the Mercantile Library.[10]

The only extant correspondence from early years of Longfellow's friendship with the Longworths is a pair of letters written in late 1851 and early 1852 by Nicholas Longworth. He, Edward Everett, and others were vetting the idea of commissioning Hiram Powers to sculpt a bust of Longfellow.[11] But starting in 1854, when "Catawba Wine" was published, correspondence is plentiful. On one occasion, Joseph wrote to Longfellow about his ten-year-old son's verses and even transcribed several.[12] The young poet, Nicholas II, graduated from Harvard and became an Ohio Supreme Court justice. He married Susan Walker, Judge Timothy Walker's daughter.[13]

In September 1855, Longfellow wrote to his publisher to ask him to be kind to Joseph Longworth, "an excellent fellow." Longfellow enclosed an autograph to be put into one of his books for Joseph.[14] That October, Joseph wrote the poet that he was shipping him bottles of still Catawba, sparkling Catawba, Isabella, and Herbemont wines. "Let me at your leisure know what you think of them," he said.

Around that same time, the Longworths visited Longfellow in Cambridge, after which Joseph wrote that he was sending "one of Mrs. Longworth's little pictures newly painted" in return for a pencil sharpener she had been given during the visit. He also sent several sea pebbles painted by his wife. One was to be forwarded to Thomas Gold Appleton, Longfellow's brother-in-law, as "a reminder that we have & shall not, forget his kindness."

"The old gentleman [his father, Nicholas I], though near seventy five, is this fall sowing grape seeds, to obtain new varieties, with all the enthusiasm of a boy, expecting to see the fruit," Joseph wrote. And his son Nicholas asked to be remembered to Charley, Longfellow's son, and Teapot, who was probably a pet of some sort. Joseph also ventured a critique on a single word that jarred on his ear in Longfellow's poem *Golden Legend,* hoping that Longfellow would not take offense. Remember, he said, that the criticism comes "from him, who not only praises your works, as creations of high art,—but who also loves them, as the children of one, whose heart is full of tenderness for everything that lives."[15]

There are several other surviving letters, including one in which Joseph thanks Longfellow for the "song to the Catawba." The letter was written in 1858, some years after the date of the poem. Most likely Longfellow sent a special copy as a gift to Nicholas I and his wife for their golden wedding anniversary, which was a much-celebrated occasion in Cincinnati on Christmas Eve, 1857.[16] Another interesting letter articulates Longfellow's opinion of Catawba wine. "I like its flavor; and though I have been called to account more than once for daring to praise it in verse, I do not resent, nor take back one word of my song. I like its wild aroma—though the French say it is *exagéré.* That is because it has more wine than their own wines."[17]

In autumn of 1862, Nicholas II visited Longfellow when he went to study at Harvard. From that visit comes one of the most popular stories about the poet and his Cincinnati friends. When young Longworth called upon Longfellow, another guest, "a busy maker of conversation," persistently referred to Longworth as Mr. Longfellow. Finally, Longfellow interrupted: "You are doing a grave injustice to my friend," he said, "in forgetting that 'tis worth that makes the man and the want of it the Fellow." The comment was much bandied about literary circles of the day.[18]

In 1861, Longfellow's wife died of burns she received when packages of her children's curls caught fire while she was sealing them with wax. Longfellow rushed to her aid and was also burned. "You know that I have always felt great respect & regard for you," Joseph wrote later, "but my feeling has become very tender since your life has been darkened by your great sorrow. For me too, the other side of the river has become brighter. I sit, & wait. Gladly at any moment will I hear the summons which permits me, leaving all else, to follow what I most love, into the unknown. That God may comfort, & bless you, is the earnest prayer of your friend, Joseph Longworth."[19]

And, yes, there was something about a visit to Cincinnati. On November 19, 1855, Joseph wrote to Longfellow from Rookwood, enclosing a letter from the secretary of the Mercantile Library. The enclosure followed up on a recent visit to Longfellow by the Mercantile's librarian and offered one hundred dollars for a talk in December or January. In his own letter, Longworth, who had been a life member of the Mercantile since 1852, commended the library as a "very worthy association," pointing out that its winter lecture series included some of the "best cultivated minds of the day." If Longfellow came to Cincinnati, he said, he would personally meet him upon his arrival and take him to his own home. "Why not bring the boys with you," he said. "Nicholas will undertake to give them 'lots of fun' in the 'pathless woods' & elsewhere."

One way or another, Joseph added, "we rely with certainty on a visit next May or June, from you with Cornelia & all her jewels." Come this winter, he said, as prologue to the spring.[20]

Unfortunately, a review of Longfellow's journals for the years in question finds him busy with daily life and turns up no reference to a visit to the Queen City. Nor have any other documents surfaced to indicate such a visit. Perhaps he intended to come to Cincinnati but simply couldn't: in the spring of 1856, his eleven-year-old son

FIGURE 8.4 City Hall window commemorating Longfellow's poetic reference to the Queen City. *Photograph by author*

Charley destroyed his thumb in a gun explosion, and that summer
he himself was so lame that he couldn't go to Europe as planned.[21]
Nevertheless, Longfellow left an enduring legacy for Cincinnati.
The "Queen City" nickname he immortalized remains in popular
usage and has been dramatized in a Tiffany stained-glass window in
Cincinnati's historic City Hall.

CHAPTER NINE

TWO TALES OF A CITY

A t Broadway and what was then Second Street in downtown Cincinnati stood the Broadway Hotel, a nineteenth-century structure that marks one of the city's most unflattering chapters of international literary history. It was there that Charles Dickens stayed when he visited the city during his 1842 tour of America.[1]

Dickens had already published *Oliver Twist, Nicholas Nickleby,* and *The Pickwick Papers,* but when he arrived in Cincinnati from Pittsburgh on the steamer *The Messenger* early on the morning of Monday, April 4, 1842, he was barely thirty years old. He, his wife, their companion, Mrs. Anne Cornelius, and his secretary, George W. Putnam, went immediately from the ship to the hotel, which was situated on one of the city's most elegant streets.[2] As one would expect, Dickens carefully observed his surroundings, noting in a letter that day,

> I have walked to the window, since I turned this page, to see what aspect the town wears. We are in a wide street: paved in the carriage-way with small white stones, and in the footway with small red tiles. The houses are for the most part one story high; some are of wood; others are of a clean white brick. Nearly all have green blinds outside every window. The principal shops over the way are, according to the inscriptions over them, a Large Bread Bakery; a Book Bindery; a Dry Goods Store; and a Carriage Repository; the last-named

looking like an exceedingly small retail coal-shed. On the pavement under our window, a black man is chopping wood; and another black man is talking (confidentially) to a pig. The public table at this hotel, and the hotel opposite, has just now finished dinner. The diners are collected on the pavement, on both sides of the way, picking their teeth, and talking. The day being warm, some of them have brought chairs into the street. Some are on three chairs; some on two; and some, in defiance of all known laws of gravity, are sitting quite comfortably on one: with three of the chair's legs, and their own two, high up in the air. The loungers, underneath our window, are talking of a great Temperance convention which comes off here tomorrow. Others, about me. Others, about England.[3]

Dickens took a somewhat jaundiced view of America during his travels, so his comments on Cincinnati are not surprising. He planned to screen out Cincinnati visitors, but before he had a chance, two local men came to call. One was Timothy Walker, the prominent local judge who had entertained Alexis de Tocqueville when he was in town. Walker was a founder of the Cincinnati Law School (the first law school in Ohio), a member of the Semi-Colon Club, a noted jurist and legal writer, and first law partner of Salmon P. Chase, later chief justice of the U.S. Supreme Court.[4]

Judge Walker invited Dickens for an impromptu tour of the city, and Dickens accepted. They visited classrooms of the city's free schools as well as a courtroom where a trial was under way. Walker also invited Dickens to attend a ball the next evening at his home, Woodland Cottage, near the corner of Grandin Road and a toll road at what was then Madison Pike.[5]

According to a woman who attended the ball, Dickens was

young and handsome, had a mellow, beautiful eye, fine brow, and abundant hair. His mouth is large and his smile so

FIGURE 9.1 Charles Dickens by Henry Dexter, plaster, at the Mercantile Library of Cincinnati. *Photograph by author*

bright it seemed to shed light and happiness all about him. His manner is easy, negligent, but not elegant. His dress was foppish; in fact, he was over dressed yet his garments were worn so easily they appeared to be a necessary part of him. He had a dark coat with lighter pantaloons; a black waistcoat embroidered with colored flowers, and about his neck covering his shirt front was a black neck cloth, also embroidered in colors, in which were placed two large diamond pins connected by a chain. A gold watch chain and a large red rose in his button hole completed his toilet. He appeared a little weary, but answered the remarks made to him—for he originated none—in an agreeable manner.

The woman who described him had arrived late to the party with several of her friends, and Dickens was already in the hall preparing to leave. Judge Walker urged him to stay to greet the new arrivals, so Dickens and his wife sat down on a sofa to wait. One young woman asked if he would give her the red rose in his buttonhole as a memento. He said he couldn't do that because the others would be jealous. Then a half dozen people clamored for the rose, so he offered to divide it among them. As he removed it from his coat, the petals fell loose to the floor. With much laughter, the young women scrambled to pick them up.[6]

Impressed with Cincinnati, Dickens wrote in a letter at the time, "Cincinnati is only fifty years old, but is a very beautiful city; I think the prettiest place I have ever seen here, except Boston. It has risen out of the forest like an Arabian-Night city; is well laid out; ornamented in the suburbs with pretty villas; and above all, for this is a very rare feature in America, has smooth turf plots and well kept gardens."[7]

He wrote to C. C. Felton of Cambridge, "I saw a good deal of Walker in Cincinnati. I like him very much." Dickens is even rumored to be in Walker's debt for one of his most memorable characters. According to an unconfirmed story, Walker told Dickens about a Cincinnati recluse who wore her wedding dress all the time because she had been jilted on her wedding day. She may be the model for Miss Havisham in *Great Expectations*.[8]

In *American Notes*, the book Dickens wrote about his 1842 tour, he was complimentary of the people he met in Cincinnati: "The society with which I mingled was intelligent, courteous and agreeable." But in private letters published in 1872 he told a different story. He complained that he had been "introduced to at least 150 first-rate bores, separately and singly [at Walker's party]. I was required to sit down by the greater part of them and talk." It was those negative comments that were widely publicized, tainting Cincinnati's literary reputation for years to come.[9]

On April 6, Dickens left Cincinnati by steamboat for Louisville, and on April 19 he returned to the city, lodging again at the Broadway Hotel. Early the next morning, he and his party took the mail coach on a macadamized road to Columbus and eventually on to New York. The group stopped for dinner at the Golden Lamb, a historic tavern still in operation in Lebanon, Ohio, and then spent twenty-three hours en route to Columbus.[10]

Dickens wrote to the Walkers from Niagara Falls and asked to be remembered to his Cincinnati friends. He also took the opportunity to take a jab at the Ohio state government. If he could, he said, he would "put the whole legislature of Ohio on wheels and make them travel backwards and forwards on that road between Columbus and Tiffin until they died—or mended it." When he returned to America in 1867, he did not stop in Cincinnati.[11]

CHAPTER TEN

ONES COMING WITH PAPERS

O n Monday evening, October 29, 1849, twelve young men, including a young bookseller destined to go on to national prominence, gathered in a dingy downtown law office to establish an organization that has nourished Cincinnati's literary life ever since.[1] The Literary Club of Cincinnati, believed to be the oldest club of its type in America still in existence, meets weekly, September to June, quietly stimulating research, literary endeavor, and a myriad of publications.[2] During its lengthy existence the all-male club has also sparked a drilling unit, an occasional duel, a funeral or two, White House get-togethers, and informal meetings with famous visitors.

Several literary clubs—the Semi-Colon Club, Daniel Drake's Buckeye Club, and the Cincinnati Literary Society, among others—had already come and gone when future librarian of Congress Ainsworth Rand Spofford and his friends organized theirs. It started with what most people would consider a bang. During its first year of existence, Spofford and several other members raised $150 in pledges to invite the popular lecturer Ralph Waldo Emerson for his first visit to the West. Emerson was guaranteed travel expenses as well as proceeds from his lectures, less the cost of renting a lecture hall. In May of 1850, he presented five lectures on the nineteenth century at the Universalist Church on Walnut Street. The lectures, "Natural Aristocracy," "Eloquence," "Spirit of the Times," "England," and "Books," were so successful that three more were added: "The Natural History of Intellect," "The

Identity of Thought and Nature," and "Instinct and Inspiration."[3] Emerson, greatly pleased, pocketed $560 for his efforts.[4]

While Emerson was in town, several literary club members, including future U.S. president Rutherford B. Hayes, called on him at Burnet House to invite him to join the club for a "confab." Emerson accepted, and on May 26 he spoke informally at the club for more than two hours on what Hayes described as "all matters from letters to raising corn and pigs." Hayes reported the visit in detail in his diary, along with descriptions of most of Emerson's Cincinnati lectures, which he attended.[5]

Emerson's forty-seventh birthday occurred while he was in town, so members of the Literary Club invited him to celebrate with an excursion to the old Indian earthworks at Fort Ancient in Warren County. According to Spofford, the party "sat under the trees on the grassy mounds on one of those delicious June days when the Earth puts on the choicest array to stir the senses to gladness." They drank Ohio wine, toured the grounds, and told stories.[6]

Based on a letter written by Spofford for the club's thirty-seventh anniversary, the Literary Club was originally organized around debate and oral discussion, with the writing of literary papers secondary.[7] However, the papers have since become the primary focus, as reflected by the slogan the club adopted years ago, "Here Comes One with a Paper," a line from Shakespeare's play *Love's Labour's Lost*. By 1970, almost ten thousand papers had been delivered at weekly meetings.[8] Today each member is expected to read aloud at least once every two years and also to contribute to the "budget," a collection of shorter pieces read to the club by the "editor of the budget" once a month. Many of the papers have been preserved, and some are now available to the public at the Cincinnati Historical Society. The body of work includes stories, history, humor, and autobiographical sketches.

Out of the club have come many books as well as other published pieces. One estimate, now considerably outdated, is that more than fourteen hundred books have been written by members.[9] Among them have been classical and biblical works by Carl W. Blegen and Nelson Glueck; travel and river stories by Clark B. Firestone; and books on geopolitics by William H. Hessler. Member Thomas Chalmers Minor wrote poetry, operas, and novels and became well known for his novel *Her Ladyship*.[10] Both "Sheridan's Ride" author T. Buchanan Read and James E. Murdoch, the man who first performed Read's poem, were members.

Hayes, who joined the club the year it was founded, apparently did little writing for the club—only a letter and one budget item—but perhaps he did his share, given that discussions and debates were the norm of his day. And he did do what few others could do: he invited the group to the White House.[11] According to his journal, all members who were available celebrated the club's twenty-ninth anniversary in Washington on October 29, 1878. Among the readings was one by Spofford, who delivered a paper by another member burlesquing the style of Emerson. The evening was one of the rare club occasions when women were invited. Mrs. Hayes was among them.[12]

Membership in the Literary Club was initially limited to twenty-five, but has been expanded through the years and now stands at one hundred. Among the many noteworthy men who have been members was another president, William Howard Taft, who joined in 1878 after graduating from Yale University. He too invited his fellow club friends to the White House. Taft wrote three club papers: "Crime and Education," "The Molly Maguires," and "Criminal Law in Hamilton County."[13]

Other distinguished names that have appeared on the club roster are U.S. Supreme Court justices, Salmon P. Chase and Alphonso Taft, and an array of senators, governors, congressmen, and cabinet members. William T. H. Howe, president of the American Book Company, was a member, as was Union general George P. McClellan, who was elected to the club just before departing for service in the war. (Apparently he failed to get his paperwork in order before he left.) Another member, Dr. John Shaw Billings, was later instrumental in the establishment of the New York Public Library and created *Index Medicus,* the surgeon general's index of medical literature of the world.[14] The artist Henry Farny was a member. He happened to live across the corridor from an early set of club rooms and would often invade the clubhouse with his friends, toting a load of beer in a wheelbarrow.[15] He donated several paintings that still decorate the club's walls.

Other prominent members have included Murat Halstead, editor of the *Cincinnati Commercial Gazette;* Frank Duveneck, a celebrated painter; John Uri Lloyd, scientist and novelist; and Congressman Charles Phelps Taft, William Howard Taft's half brother and owner/editor of the *Cincinnati Times-Star.*

The club has had many important visitors since the precedent was set with Ralph Waldo Emerson. Visitors are never burdened with formal remarks, but they are usually asked to speak informally after the readings of the evening and to sign the club's guest book. The visits of Mark Twain and Robert Frost will be described elsewhere, but other prominent visitors have included playwright and wit Oscar Wilde; anthropologist and author Loren Eiseley; poets Randall Jarrell, Stephen Spender, John Betjeman, and Karl Shapiro; and Anglo-Jewish writer and activist Israel Zangwill. Alex Haley, author of *Roots: The Saga of an American Family,* and writer, orator, and educator Booker T. Washington also met with the club. Washington gave a much-applauded talk on the Tuskegee Institute around the turn of the nineteenth century.

The club has been situated in more than a dozen locations, but since June 30, 1930, it has resided in a two-story red brick building at 500 East Fourth Street. The building was acquired through a favorable arrangement with the city's prominent Taft family, which lived in the nearby home once owned by Nicholas Longworth. Little has changed in the club through the years, including the regular meeting schedule, the antique- and art-filled rooms, and the strictly all-male

FIGURE 10.1 The Literary Club of Cincinnati, 500 E. Fourth Street. *Photograph by Louis E. Enzweiler*

membership policy. At the 150th anniversary celebration it was suggested that it might be time to rethink the membership policy, but the idea met with strong opposition and the subject was dropped.[16] (Fortunately, Cincinnati women took matters into their own hands more than a hundred years ago and started their own club, Noon Day. Other such clubs have been started since.[17])

Nevertheless, there have been some changes over the years. A diversity of occupations, including academia, journalism, medicine, religion, and business, is still represented, but the average age of the membership has increased considerably since men in their twenties founded the club. Now one of the favorite sayings at the club is "A 'budget' reading should be just long enough to keep forty-five old men awake for forty-five minutes." In the early days, members met on Saturday nights, but now the meetings are on Monday nights. Drinks and dinner preceded the readings at one time, but rowdiness and heckling of readers eventually caused the club to postpone drinking, eating, and smoking until afterward. (Things calmed down a bit during Prohibition, so it is now possible to at least enjoy a prereading drink.[18])

The club has learned through the years how to avoid the type of controversy that prompted members to destroy the minutes of several Civil War–era meetings, which included harsh words and threats of duels. Now new members quickly learn that commerce is to be left outside club walls and that papers featuring religious or political sentiments are not welcome. They are also instructed on the proper protocol for the reading of papers. Readers are not permitted to say a single word beyond their written presentations, and listeners may neither ask questions nor make comments during or immediately following the readings. Everyone who has made a sincere effort with his writing is simply applauded, and then complimented informally over dinner.

Of course, it takes leadership and not just rules to maintain a civil society. Back in 1957, one man described the responsibilities that come with the presidency: "The presiding officer's most important duty is to announce the essayist, warn off unanointed ones before business meetings, and in his parliamentary ignorance, make as few mistakes as possible during such club curses as the 'shall we meet on Christmas Eve?' debate."[19]

Actually, with few exceptions, the club seems to have generated strong esprit de corps throughout much of its history. One of the most often told tales is from the Civil War era, when members agreed after the attack on Fort Sumter to volunteer for military service. They formed an informal drill unit that came to be known as the "Burnet Rifles," and soon almost all the members entered the armed forces of the United States. (One member may have joined the Confederacy, but that story isn't readily available.) Even in peacetime, however, a supportive atmosphere and strong club loyalty have been typical. For example, one member who joined the club in 1885, Dr. Lawrence Carr, bequeathed the organization eighty thousand dollars on condition that the club hold his funeral at the clubhouse and carry his name permanently on the roster.[20] (His wishes are still being honored.) Another member who had the misfortune to be hospitalized at the time of a club banquet was so committed to the organization that he had himself dressed in a tuxedo with a carnation in the lapel and carried to the banquet on a stretcher. He was returned to the hospital afterwards.[21]

One member opined in a paper that there must be a Celestial Branch of the Literary Club, where all earthly members in good standing are automatically admitted after death.[22] Whether this is true or not, the club seems to go beyond endurance, and to thrive, encouraging a literate community in a day when many people can't spell without spell-check or write anything other than e-mails and tweets. It is even difficult to resign from the Literary Club without doing so in writing. One man tried back in 1891, recruiting a friend to submit his resignation for him at the evening's meeting. The message was duly delivered, but generated such heated debate that the fellow was let off the hook only after a quick-witted pundit pointed out that there was no evidence from his club contributions that the man could write. Written resignation was waived.[23]

CHAPTER ELEVEN

J. B. POND'S SERVANT

Samuel Clemens, or Mark Twain, as he came to be known, was twenty years old when he arrived in Cincinnati by train late in October 1856 and got a job as a typesetter at Wrightson and Co., a thriving establishment in what was then the center of western printing. In Keokuk, Iowa, where he had worked at a print shop with his brother, he had dreamed of going to South America, but the trip fell through. He happened upon a fifty-dollar bill on the street one day, and when no one stepped forward to claim it, bought a ticket for Cincinnati and left town. "I felt that I must take that money out of danger," he liked to say.[1]

For many years the only known Twain connection with Cincinnati was the proverbial, but probably apocryphal, quip, "When the end of the world comes, I want to be in Cincinnati—it is always twenty years behind the times." Twain was somewhat mysterious about his six months in the city; he mentioned it less often than other periods of his life. Likewise, Cincinnatians have never paid much attention to his Cincinnati stay. No historic plaque marks the site where he worked; there are no restored, or even salvaged, homes; no one conducts special walking tours. Only in modern times has a diligent scholar, William Baker, shed light on the period.

In an article published in the late 1970s, Baker referenced a section in Twain's 1924 *Autobiography* in which he describes his life in a Cincinnati boardinghouse as filled mostly with "commonplace" or "oppressively uninteresting people." There was one notable exception, a Scotsman referred to as Macfarlane. Baker believed "Macfarlane" was actually John J. McFarland, a fellow printer at Wrightson who was twice Twain's age. Twain described the two as "comrades from the start" and said he spent evenings by the wood fire in McFarland's room, "listening in comfort to his tireless talk and to the dulled complainings of the winter storms." Although McFarland had little schooling, he claimed to have learned every word in the English dictionary. Twain said he was never able to trip him up.

Twain's views on religious, moral, and philosophical matters are said to have been influenced by McFarland, who, among other things, propounded ideas about evolution that were ahead of his time.[2]

Significantly, it was in Cincinnati that Twain first tried his hand at professional writing. He is believed to have authored a sketch about a boardinghouse and a character named Mr. Blathers, who bears a striking resemblance to MacFarlane. Scholars think Twain sent the sketch to his brother in Keokuk, where it was published under the signature "L" in the *Keokuk Post*. He is also said to have published several letters from Cincinnati in the *Post* under the name Thomas Jefferson Snodgrass.[3] These have become known as "the Snodgrass letters."

Although Twain had worked in printing since his father died when he was eleven, he concluded during his Cincinnati days that printing wasn't for him. He may have had to work harder at Wrightson than with his brother in Iowa, but more likely the problem was that his Cincinnati job fed his dream of riverboating. During his tenure, Wrightson printed two thousand copies of *James' River Guide*, considered the bible for river pilots, and Twain reportedly memorized it. Wrightson also printed Q. Walton's *History of John A. Muriel*, a book that impressed Twain so much he quoted extensively from it in *Life on the Mississippi*. And, of course, he lived and worked only a short distance from the busy Ohio River boat landing, which would have piqued his river interests.

On April 15, 1857, Twain abandoned the printing business for good and booked passage on the steamboat *Paul Jones*, moving westward down the Ohio toward the Mississippi. Ostensibly, he was headed for New Orleans and from there to Brazil, where he planned to collect coca for the cocaine trade and make his fortune. Along the way, however, he approached the ship's pilot, a man named Horace Bixby, about a job and got himself hired on as an apprentice. For the next four years, he plied the Mississippi on ten different riverboats. The rest is literary history.[4]

So where did Twain live and work in Cincinnati? In the 1857 *Williams' City Directory,* he is listed in a special section of "alterations, omissions, removals" as living at 76 Walnut. Apparently he lived there only briefly before moving to a boardinghouse at nearby 145 West Third Street. Both sites have been lost to riverfront development.[5]

Wrightson and Co., the printing establishment where he worked, was just across the street from the Mercantile Library, not far from the gaping ramp for the underground parking garage at the rear of what was then 167 Walnut.

Twain returned to the city only once. In 1885, almost thirty years after he had lived there, he came through on a reading tour with his friend George W. Cable. The two spoke on January 2 and 3 in three appearances at Odeon Hall. Cable, a small, well-dressed man with dark hair and a long, pointed beard, appeared first on the program in the initial performance, and, after being introduced to the large crowd, sat down at a table onstage to wait while latecomers were seated. According to the *Cincinnati Enquirer,* he "had the look of an overworked student who was cultivating brain at the expense of physique." After his performance, which the *Enquirer* described as dramatic rather than humorous, Twain wandered in. In contrast to Cable, he was "tall, awkward, gestureless, with a shock head of iron-gray hair and a deeply-furrowed, tired face." He chatted confidently with the audience in a Down East nasal tone. Every sentence "concealed a mirth provoker of some kind," the paper said.[6] After talking at length, he wandered off.

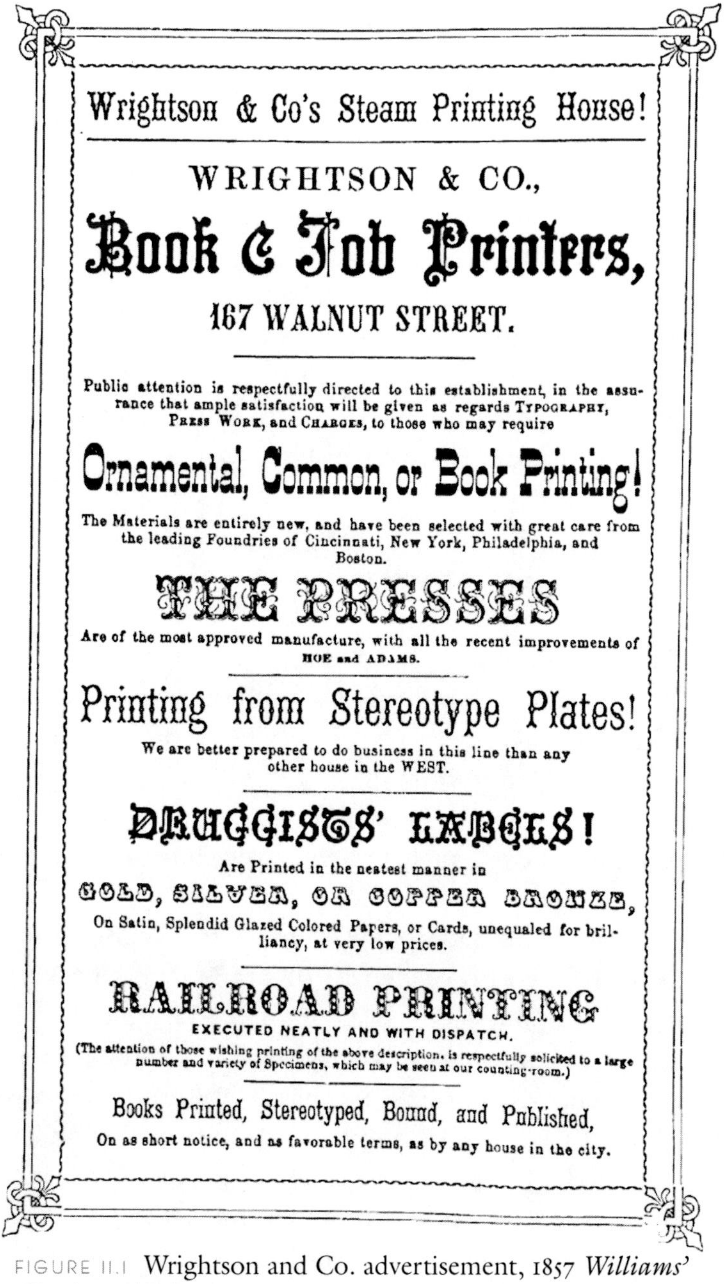

Wrightson & Co's Steam Printing House!

WRIGHTSON & CO.,

Book & Job Printers,

167 WALNUT STREET.

Public attention is respectfully directed to this establishment, in the assurance that ample satisfaction will be given as regards TYPOGRAPHY, PRESS WORK, and CHARGES, to those who may require

Ornamental, Common, or Book Printing!

The Materials are entirely new, and have been selected with great care from the leading Foundries of Cincinnati, New York, Philadelphia, and Boston.

THE PRESSES

Are of the most approved manufacture, with all the recent improvements of HOE and ADAMS.

Printing from Stereotype Plates!

We are better prepared to do business in this line than any other house in the WEST.

DRUGGISTS' LABELS!

Are Printed in the neatest manner in

GOLD, SILVER, OR COPPER BRONZE,

On Satin, Splendid Glazed Colored Papers, or Cards, unequaled for brilliancy, at very low prices.

RAILROAD PRINTING

EXECUTED NEATLY AND WITH DISPATCH.

(The attention of those wishing printing of the above description, is respectfully solicited to a large number and variety of Specimens, which may be seen at our counting-room.)

Books Printed, Stereotyped, Bound, and Published,

On as short notice, and as favorable terms, as by any house in the city.

FIGURE II.1 Wrightson and Co. advertisement, 1857 *Williams' Cincinnati Directory*

In the several appearances during his stay, Twain presented "Certain Personal Episodes" and "Why I Lost the Editorship" and read a chapter from *Huckleberry Finn,* which was about to be published in the United States. He also gave what was described as a sidesplitting rendition of a dueling incident he had experienced in the West. According to the *Enquirer,* the engagements were financially successful and the audiences went away pleased.[7]

More interesting in some ways than the formal performances, however, were Twain and Cable's other activities while they were in town. At 11 p.m. after the January 2 performance, the *Enquirer* interviewed them in the dining room of the St. Nicholas Hotel at Fourth and Vine Streets, where they were registered as J. B. Pond's servants, ostensibly to avoid autograph seekers and other interlopers.[8] Mr. Cable "was getting away with some chocolate ice cream," and Twain had a half-empty bottle of Bass pale ale before him. Their managers, J. B. and Ozias W. Pond, were with them. "Glad to see you, *Enquirer,*" Twain said as he held out his hand and introduced everyone.

"Thought you might be able to say something interesting," the reporter said. "You have been both interviewed probably on every conceivable subject, so if you will just rattle away and talk about anything it will answer. You know how it is yourself."

"You should not expect a fellow to be very interesting after two hours on the platform," Twain said.

"You are not expected to say much," the reporter replied. Nevertheless, the two proceeded to discuss Twain's background as a reporter, his opinion of the writer Bret Harte, and which of Twain's books he considered his favorite. (He said he didn't have one, but *Innocents Abroad* paid the best royalties.) After a while, Twain gazed sadly at the now-empty bottle in front of him and announced that he had to go to bed. After he departed, the reporter continued to chat with Cable, who mentioned that he and Twain fought constantly. He said he thought he could take Twain in four three-minute rounds with soft gloves.[9]

Twain and Cable did indeed get into a fight while in town, during a visit to the Literary Club. Per the club's traditions, the two made informal remarks, and then Twain announced that he would never come to the club with Cable again, because Cable drank so much "there isn't enough left for me." Cable, a teetotaler, took offense and required much cajoling and a long cooling-down period before he could be persuaded that Twain was only joking.[10]

CHAPTER TWELVE

THE DEAN AND THE QUEEN

Though W. D. Howells, dean of late nineteenth- and early twentieth-century American letters, lived in Cincinnati only briefly, the city is not a mere footnote in his life; it's a chapter.

Author of more than a hundred books and an important voice in the school of realism, Howells was born March 1, 1837, in Martinsville (now Martins Ferry), Ohio, and he spent almost a quarter of a century in various parts of the Buckeye State. His father moved his wife and eight children to Hamilton and then Dayton, Eureka Mills near Xenia, Columbus, Ashtabula, and Jefferson, as he scratched out a living writing, publishing newspapers, and clerking for the Ohio legislature. In 1856, he took young Will and his sister to Columbus, where Will, who had grown up setting type and doing other editorial chores for his father, was to help put together a "Letter from Columbus" for the *Cincinnati Gazette*. The senior Howells would gather the news; the junior would write it up.

Howells later described Columbus as a "metropolis of the mind" with opportunities to read from the riches of the state library, study the classics, and observe life in Ohio's capital. He lived with his father and sister at Goodale House, an "old fashioned hotel on the northward stretch of High Street" in the business district. His father had a prime desk on the floor of the state legislature, and after he and his son had assembled a column from the news of the day, they sent it off to Cincinnati by express agent in time for the next day's newspaper. Initially, they signed the letters "Jeffersonian," a pseudonym his father used, but Howells quickly learned to do the whole job himself and adopted his own pseudonym, "Chispa," after a rogue servant in a poem by Longfellow.

Howells had an opportunity to attend legislative social functions during his first winter in Columbus, and later recalled a ball and banquet for the opening of the new statehouse. Instead of enjoying the party, as most people his age might have, Howells holed up in a corner writing his daily report. "I was there as the representative of a great Cincinnati newspaper," he said, "and I cared more to please its management than to take any such part as I might in the festivity."[1]

And he did please the management. When the legislative session ended in 1857, a man by the name of Edmund B. Babb called on him in Columbus to offer him a job as city editor of the *Cincinnati Gazette*. Babb's voice was so hushed when he made the offer that Howells wasn't sure "that the incredible thing he was proposing was really expressed to me."[2]

The title of the new job was apparently more glamorous than the job itself. The duties consisted primarily of taking charge of the local reporting in Cincinnati. This meant relocation, but the salary was wonderful: one thousand dollars a year, or double what he was making in Columbus. It was too good to pass up; Will agreed to give it a try.[3]

Howells had never lived away from his family, but he had some familiarity with Cincinnati because he had visited his uncles, who regularly plied the Ohio in their sidewheel steamers, while they were in port there. From time to time, he and his mother had traveled out of Cincinnati as guests on his uncles' boats to visit relatives in Pittsburgh. And he had probably heard about Cincinnati from his father, too, because the elder Howells had spent a year reading medicine and working as a printer there.[4]

To Howells, Cincinnati was the big city; when he arrived in March of 1857, it was ten times larger than Columbus. At first he was impressed and happy. According to a letter he wrote to his brother on April 10, while he was still settling in, he liked the living quarters he shared with his editor and enjoyed boarding at a restaurant, which he did for about three dollars a week. He had "grown fond of this big bustling city. The everlasting and furious rushing up and down, and to and fro, pleases me," he said, "and I like nothing better than to stroll about the streets alone, and stealthily contemplate the shop windows and orange stands, and speculate on the people I meet." He also went down to the river nearly every day, searching for a glimpse of his uncles' steamboats (he hadn't spotted them at this point).

Howells started out at the *Gazette* correcting manuscripts and doing other editorial chores, but expected to gradually work into the reporting job.[5] Unfortunately for Cincinnati, it didn't turn out that way. "One night's round of the police stations with the other reporters satisfied me that I was not meant for that work, and I attempted it no farther." Lafcadio Hearn would later relish covering the sordid, grisly underbelly of the city, but Howells abhorred it.[6]

Howells also got homesick and lonely. Away from his friends and large family and prone to periods of what today might be called depression or anxiety, he floundered as he walked the unfamiliar streets and ate alone in restaurants. Regrettably, he didn't run into Samuel Clemens, who was working nearby during part of the time he was in town. The two had much in common and might have struck up the kind of friendship they would form later, perhaps changing the course of their own, and Cincinnati's, literary history. As it was, the kindly Babb was Howells's only real friend, and although he adjusted his young protégé's duties as best he could to give him the type of work he wanted, he had no suitable opening. By fall, Howells had returned to Columbus.

Although brief, Howells's tenure in Cincinnati was significant in several ways. Certainly he learned something about himself and his writing interests through his experiences there. He also learned an important life lesson through a particular incident. A prominent

FIGURE 12.1 Cincinnati Gazette Building, as shown in *Richardson, the Architect and The Cincinnati Chamber of Commerce Building* (Cincinnati: Cincinnati Astronomical Society, 1914)

citizen came to the *Gazette* office with his lawyer one night to ask that his illicit affair be kept out of the newspaper to avoid ruining both his and his female friend's good names. After considerable debate, the editors agreed to withhold the information. However, the next morning the story broke in a competitive newspaper. "But," Howells said, "I cannot feel even yet that the beauty of our merciful decision was marred by this mockery of fate, or that the cause of virtue was served by it, and I think that if I had been wiser than I was then I would have remained in the employ offered me, and learned in the school of reality the many lessons of human nature which it could have taught me."[7]

Howells didn't live in Cincinnati long, but, with plenty of time on his hands, he carefully observed local life. For example, he amused himself as he "overate" his restaurant meals by listening to the waiters as they called their orders into the kitchen below. The phrase he liked best was for a double order of corncakes: "Indians, six on a plate." He also closely observed female clerks and shopgirls as they dined alone, and used those observations, and perhaps others, to draw realistic characters for some of the novels he wrote later.

Nor was Howells done writing for Cincinnati audiences. He continued to do an occasional "sketch" for Babb and planned to take up his old column again until he got sick and his father had to take over. The column was later given to Whitelaw Reid, who went on to become a correspondent for the *Gazette* during the Civil War and Horace Greeley's successor as editor of the *New York Tribune*. Reid and Howells became good friends and spent a particularly memorable Thanksgiving together in Columbus, playing charades and eating turkey at the home of Salmon P. Chase, the distinguished Cincinnati lawyer who was then serving as governor and later became President Lincoln's secretary of the treasury.[8] The Thanksgiving occasion drew Howells into Columbus's social life.[9]

In 1860, Will set off for what might be called his Niagara Tour, a swing through Canada and New England for a book on industries of the East. There again, Cincinnati proved instrumental: the *Cincinnati Gazette* was one of two newspapers that agreed to accept travel stories from the tour. Those stories helped finance his trip and allowed him to do the kind of writing he wanted to do. (He wasn't excited about the book on manufacturing.) He published seven columns entitled "Glimpses of Summer Travel" in the *Gazette,* writing under the Chispa name.[10] "I greet you, Cincinnatians, from this beautiful city of the North," he wrote from Montreal, "where I button my woolen coat, with a calm feeling of October comfort in the act—I greet you that swelter and fry up Fourth street and down Vine, and offer you my sincerest compassion."[11] From material gathered on this northern trip, he collaborated with Mark Twain and several others to publish *The Niagara Book,* which makes frequent reference to his chores for "that Cincinnati newspaper."[12]

The Niagara Tour was important to Howells for a variety of reasons, among them the opportunity it gave him to meet many of the best-known literary figures of his day. Some years later, when he was assistant editor of the *Atlantic Monthly*, he assembled his early newspaper letters, thinking he might make a book out of them. He finally decided against the project, but did draw on the material for two of his novels, *Their Wedding Journey* and *A Chance Acquaintance*. [13]

Although Howells was a journalist and prose writer much of his life, his first love was poetry, and Cincinnati figures briefly in that story as well. One of his earliest publications was *Old Winter*, a piece his father slipped into the *Ohio State Journal* without his knowledge. The fifteen-year-old Will didn't comment in his diary on the poem's initial publication, but he did express joy when he saw it reprinted in two newspapers, one of which was the *Cincinnati Commercial*.[14] In 1860, he published his first book, *Poems of Two Friends*, with John James Piatt, who later worked for the *Cincinnati Commercial* and the *Cincinnati Chronicle*, reviewed books for the *Cincinnati Enquirer*, and published several books of poetry with Cincinnati publishers.[15]

Another Cincinnati publication with which Howells developed a relationship was the *Dial*, a transcendental magazine that attracted a number of well-known Eastern writers, including Ralph Waldo Emerson and Louisa May Alcott. "Never shall I forget the day when he [Howells] came to see us in Cincinnati," editor and founder Moncure D. Conway wrote in his *Autobiography*. "There was about him a sincerity and simplicity, a repose of manner along with a maturity of strength, surprising in a countenance so young—and I must add, beautiful—that I knew perfectly well my new friend had a great career before him." The two developed a lasting friendship.[16]

In 1861, Howells secured a post as consul to Venice and, during his four-year tour of duty there, married the distant cousin of a Cincinnati lawyer and congressman, the future president of the United States Rutherford B. Hayes. Elinor Mead and Howells had met in Columbus while Elinor was a houseguest of Hayes during Hayes's tenure in the Ohio legislature.[17]After Howells returned from abroad, he looked for a newspaper job in Boston, and after he was unsuccessful, he left his family there while he continued his search in Ohio. No details are available, but apparently he sought work not just in Columbus, but also in Cincinnati and Cleveland.[18] When he failed to find a job, he returned to the East, where he stayed, eventually becoming famous as the editor of the *Nation,* the *Atlantic Monthly,* and *Cosmopolitan.* He also wrote a popular column for *Harper's Weekly* and published a large number of books, including the well-known *Rise of Silas Lapham.*

In later life, Howells returned again and again to the subject matter of Ohio. Among his memoirs were *A Boy's Town,* the story of his life in Hamilton in the 1840s; *My Year in a Log Cabin,* about his family's experiences at Eureka Mills; and two books featuring details of his Cincinnati experiences, *Years of My Youth* and *My Literary Passions.* He also wrote several novels that drew upon his Midwestern roots, among them *The Kentons, The Shadow of a Dream, The Coast of Bohemia,* and *Indian Summer,* which tapped his knowledge of the famous artists from Cincinnati who studied in Florence and Venice. Other works included *Ohio Stories,* which featured accounts of many of Cincinnati's best-known figures (Harriet Beecher Stowe, the Cary sisters, Nicholas Longworth, and others); and *Sketch of the Life and Character of Rutherford B. Hayes.* And he suggested, edited, wrote the introduction for, and completed his father's *Recollections of Life in Ohio, from 1813 to 1840.*

Howells clearly cherished his Ohio roots and particularly valued his time in Hamilton, which he described as the "gladdest" place of his childhood.[19] Throughout his life he tested new fountain pens by writing, "William Dean Howells, Hamilton, Butler County, Ohio."[20] Hamilton, situated about thirty miles from Cincinnati, now has a walking/driving tour of twelve local sights connected with Howells.

FIGURE 12.2 William D. Howells seated at his desk, ca. 1919. *Photograph by Jessie Tarbox Beals, The Schlesinger Library, Radcliffe Institute, Harvard University*

The schoolchildren of Cincinnati planted a tree in Howells's honor in 1882. He couldn't come for the occasion but asked the school principal to convey his "very sincere thanks for the great honor they have done in planting a tree in recognition of what I have attempted in literature. I hope they did not forget that I am myself a Buckeye; and that the Miami woods were all akin to me once."[21]

When four hundred celebrities gathered in New York in 1912 to mark Howells's seventy-fifth birthday, Cincinnati was represented by one of its favorite sons, President William Howard Taft. In deference to Taft's presidential schedule, the event was moved from Howells's actual birthday on March 1 to March 2.[22]

One final note: Howells came back to Cincinnati in 1899 as part of a Midwestern tour. On what seems to have been his first visit to the city since early adulthood, he lectured on "Novels" at the Odeon as a benefit for charity patients at a local hospital. He was introduced by his old Cincinnati friend John James Piatt, who took the opportunity to comment on the book of poetry he and Howells had published almost forty years earlier, which, he said, had sunk into "oblivion" as soon as it appeared.

Among the people Howells met while he was in town was John B. Peaslee, the Cincinnati educator who had started Authors Grove. Howells enquired about the tree that had been planted in his honor in Eden Park and was pleased it was still "flourishing." Newspaper coverage of his visit included a phrenological reading of his head by a local psychic.[23]

CHAPTER THIRTEEN

A HAIRDRESSER TELLING ALL

I n October 1859, two Cincinnati newspapers engaged in a polite contretemps over a handsome new book just gone on
sale at Rickey, Mallory and Co. booksellers on Main Street. The
Cincinnati Daily Gazette gave the local author a positive review,
calling the book "bold, if not very polished."[1] The *Daily Commercial* insisted the *Gazette* was mistaken: "The innate vulgarity, the
prying curiosity, the offensive coarseness of the class to which the
author belongs, are fitly and fully illustrated in its pages."[2]

The book was *A Hairdresser's Experience in High Life,* and
although it was published anonymously, everyone, including the
newspapers, knew exactly who wrote it. The author was Mrs. Eliza
Potter, an African American who "combed" for the highest ranks
of society. Her book, an account of her travels, experiences, and
observations over several decades, details the faults of nineteenth-
century society so forthrightly that Fanny Trollope's decidedly
more famous *Domestic Manners* seems petty in comparison.

Instead of stopping at such trivialities as hogs in the streets and
neighbors who arrive unannounced, Mrs. Potter heaps tale upon
tale of hypocrisy, greed, callousness, social climbing, swindling,
gluttony, child neglect, sexual infidelity, and even thievery. She tells
of a man who treats his wife devotedly in public but pinches her
and tortures her "in every way imaginable" in private. She reports
on women who steal opera cloaks at a party, knowing the servants
will be blamed. She describes a society so cruel that a neighbor

hung "an old dress, with needles, thimble, spools of cotton, scissors and everything belonging to a dress-maker" on a woman's doorknob to remind her "from what she had sprung."[3]

Although her book is not a polemic on race, Potter details the savagery of slavery and describes widespread miscegenation, implying hypocrisy on the part of many segments of society, including Northerners, who, she says, sometimes treat African Americans worse than slaveholders do. No one is safe from her critical eye. "I remember a colored woman who was raised in Cincinnati . . . ; she is now a slave-holder in the city of New Orleans; the most tyrannical, overbearing, cruel task-mistress that ever existed; so you can see color makes no difference, the propensities are the same."[4]

To be sure, Potter doesn't name names, being careful to stick to initials and dashes: "a family named B——," "Mrs. W.," and "Col. H.," for example. And the book ranges far beyond the city of Cincinnati. Long portions cover lengthy stays in London and Paris as well as in various parts of the United States, including Saratoga, Natchez, and New Orleans, where she spent many social seasons dressing "twenty-five heads" in an evening.[5] She also skips around in her account, making it difficult to determine the precise time frames she's discussing.

Even so, one guesses that many of her clients easily recognized themselves and their friends. In fact, today, more than 150 years later, "Mr. L.," Cincinnati's wealthy Nicholas Longworth, is readily identifiable. Potter claims to have worked for Mr. L. at one point and praises him in glowing terms. She describes his golden wedding anniversary celebration, an elaborate affair for which she did Mrs. L.'s hair, and notes some of the artists he generously supported.[6]

Eliza Potter, or Iangy as apparently she was nicknamed, was on hand for many important events through the years, which she makes a point of citing. In London she witnessed the baptism of the Prince of Wales. In Saratoga Springs she celebrated the news of the laying of the Transatlantic Telegraph Cable. In Cincinnati, she observed the openings of both the Burnet House (1850) and Pike's Opera House (1859). Inevitably, her accounts offer a personal twist. For the opening of Pike's, for instance, the ever-principled Iangy refuses to dress the hair of women who plan to attend the concert leading up to the opening, but feel too "sanctimonious" to attend the opera itself. "I told them I was actually afraid to comb any one that was so good that the sight of a green curtain frightened them, for such good people were unusual."[7]

She also reports on cholera epidemics, hotel fires, transatlantic journeys, bathing on the beaches of Newport, and a wide assortment of dinners, parties, clambakes, and other events experienced by the people of the day.

Who was this brave African American woman who dared speak out in pre–Civil War Cincinnati, even at the risk of her own livelihood? Why did she write her book, and what was the impact of it? It is difficult to know the answers to these questions, because Mrs. Potter focuses on observations and opinions about others, rather than on the particulars of her own life. Public records discovered to date are limited in scope, and no other writings by her are extant. Here is what can be pieced together:

Our author's parents and maiden name are unknown, and her birth date and birthplace are uncertain. She says she was raised in New York, but she may have been an escaped slave from Virginia.[8] By her own account, she went out at an early age to earn her living "in the service of people of *ton*," meaning fashionable people, but soon realized she had a "vagabond disposition, and loved change." She wanted "to see the world—and especially the *Western* world," so she went traveling. She ended up marrying in Buffalo, but after a few years left her husband to travel on.[9] Whether the two ever reunited for any period, whether they divorced, or whether he died is unknown. We do know she was Mrs. Johnson at one point.[10]

Potter visited Canada and then went west, probably arriving in Cincinnati in the 1830s.[11] She worked as a domestic servant or governess in the early years and traveled with various employers to Europe and other parts of the United States. In Paris she decided to study several crafts, settling on hairdressing as her occupation. Her choice proved fortuitous because she loved it and was good at it. According to her, she satisfied all her hairdressing customers except "a few meddlesome persons, who were jealous because some one else looked better than they did."[12] From time to time she even taught hairdressing. In 1860, she had a nineteen-year-old apprentice living with her in Cincinnati.[13]

Potter seems to have thought of Cincinnati as home for three decades, despite being gone for long periods because of her employment. In 1853, she married Howard Potter, a widower with two children: Kate, born about 1849, and James, born about 1851.[14]

Eliza Potter is listed in the Cincinnati *Williams' City Directory* for 1857, 1858, 1860, and 1861, and her husband is listed for 1859 (he was a porter). The Potters lived at 6 Home Street, where they owned their own home, valued at $2,000. They also had personal property worth $400, making them well off in their day.[15] Mrs. Potter says she wrote her book under her own "vine and fig tree" in Cincinnati.[16] She was even prominent enough to become a trustee of the city's Colored Orphan Asylum, which was located in her neighborhood.[17]

According to the 1860 federal census for the city of Cincinnati, Potter was a "mulatto," which suggests she was light skinned.[18] Although she behaved as though she were freeborn, she did endure a dramatic imprisonment while living in Cincinnati. She was accused of helping a Kentucky slave escape, and "thousands" of people followed her when she was taken to an Ohio River ferryboat to be turned over to Kentucky authorities. She spent three months in a Kentucky jail awaiting trial, but refused to confess. She spoke out in her own defense in court and was finally freed.[19]

Potter reports a number of other experiences in Cincinnati. She plied still-familiar streets such as Race, Elm, and Plum when she visited clients in the East and West Ends. She worked for a time as a ladies' maid at the well-known Broadway Hotel. And she noted the excitement of several hundred boys with sleds who took over downtown thoroughfares after a snowstorm. She also mentions the popular Menter's Band, Smith and Nixon's Hall, the Hungarian revolutionary Louis Kossuth's visit to the city, and many goings on at Burnet House. (According to her, any woman who wanted to raise her status in Cincinnati had simply to take up residence at Burnet House and cultivate the right acquaintances. Patronizing certain dressmakers was important too.[20])

Potter admits to a "fiery temper" in her youth and offers many negative observations about Cincinnati, but positive ones as well. For example, she points out that easterners often think western people "wild" until they visit "our Queen City of the West." She is happy to report that one visitor regretted not heeding her hairdresser's advice to buy an elegant headdress for a local party. She laughs at eastern ladies who come to the city and discover that "the people are not so green, nor are wealthy husbands so easily picked up as they think."[21]

Mrs. Potter's book is part memoir, part picaresque travel chronicle, and part what she saw as simply a way to share what she had learned from an exceptional life. "It may perhaps be considered presumptive for one in my humble sphere of life to think of writing a book; but, influenced by the earnest persuasions of many ladies and gentlemen, I have at last concluded that I must just as well note down a few of my experiences for their amusement as not," she writes in "The Author's Appeal" at the beginning of the book. She points out that her avocation takes her into the upper classes of society and that "there reign as many elements of misery as the world can produce."[22]

Potter's story as she tells it is not of the traditional rags to riches, but of a self-made woman who achieved a certain wealth and celebrity. She is clearly pleased to present her accomplishments. For instance, she describes a train fire in which her baggage, filled with half her clothing, is burned. She is amused by top railroad personnel who are skeptical about the value of her losses, asserting that their wives don't own outfits nearly as expensive as hers. She persists in her demands until the head of the railroad gives her $300 for her ten silk dresses.[23]

Potter makes a convincing case for her hard-won social expertise, and, in general, her observations are evenhanded and practical, even if her stories seem a bit gossipy by today's standards. "People never lose anything by being polite, especially to those in whose power they have placed themselves," she says. "I like to work for a lady who puts confidence in me and treats me accordingly as I merit," she asserts. When she is advised that her patrons may stop doing business with her because she dresses too well, she admonishes the speaker: "I told him I worked for my patrons for their money, and when I earned and got it, I did not ask them how I should spend it, or anything else connected with it, what I should eat, drink or wear, or how I should dispose of my money."[24]

However, Mrs. Potter's book also represents a sort of veiled threat, as one critic has pointed out.[25] Mrs. Potter obviously knows a great deal about the people she describes, and she can certainly tell more if she chooses. After all, as she says, "the hair-dresser is everywhere chatted with, and confided to."[26]

Potter's book is significant in part because it provides a striking example of one of the nation's earliest entrepreneurs. The University of Cincinnati's Sharon G. Dean has called *A Hairdresser's Experience in High Life* "the earliest portrait of the rising black middle and upper middle class."[27] Xiomara Santamarina of the University of Michigan has noted Potter's "entrepreneurial, lucrative work as one of the nation's first hairdressers, at a moment when the production of white, bourgeois femininity was just emerging as an income-generating beauty industry." Santamarina goes on to suggest that the book extends "beyond the boundaries of the travel narrative to incorporate an ethnographic study of a social class, depicting rich rather than poor subjects."[28]

Potter refuses to see herself as a victim, either as a woman or as an African American. Rather, she manages to position herself as an expert of sorts. "I have seen so much of human nature in my humble position that I can, by looking at a man or woman, tell what they are," she says.[29]

Eliza's husband, Howard, died in 1860, and she left for Niagara, New York, shortly afterward, taking with her, according to the Niagara federal census, her hairdresser apprentice, Louisa Taylor, and her stepdaughter, listed as Catherine.[30] Apparently Eliza was living in New York in 1880 and in Saratoga Springs in 1889, and she may have died in Rye, New York, in 1893.[31] No one knows whether she lost her Cincinnati clients because of the book, whether she ever went back to Europe, or whether any other writing survives in some yet-to-be identified form. Today, however, Eliza Potter is returning to the public eye. In the late 1980s or early 1990s, Sharon Dean called Potter's book to the attention of educator and scholar Henry Louis Gates Jr., who reprinted it in 1991 as an addition to his series the Schomburg Library of Nineteenth-Century Black Women Writers. In 2003, the Public Library of Cincinnati and Hamilton County included Potter as one of "Three Voices from Cincinnati's Past" in a digital presentation for the city's Tall Stacks celebration.[32] And in 2009, Santamarina published a new, fully annotated edition of *A Hairdresser's Experience in High Life* with the most extensive biographical detail yet. One imagines that Mrs. Potter would be pleased.

CHAPTER FOURTEEN

THE NEW JOURNALIST

The man admitted he didn't like the boy, and he hardly knew who he was or why he'd been sent to him. Furthermore, he had plenty of responsibilities of his own. Could he be blamed? When an unattractive, penniless teenager with a pearl eye arrived in Cincinnati in 1869 to look up the relation of a family servant, he had little to recommend him. The would-be benefactor gave him the money his relatives had sent for him and, after three visits, never saw him again.[1] The teenager slept in doorways and boxes and scrapped for food. However, eight years later, when Lafcadio Hearn moved on to New Orleans, Martinique, and Japan, he had already made a definitive literary mark.

Born in 1850 of an Irish surgeon serving in the British army and a Greek woman from the island of Lefkas, Hearn had a difficult beginning. His parents took him to Dublin as a baby, but soon they split, and he was abandoned to the care of his father's aunt. By the time he was seven, both parents had left the country, and he never saw either of them again.[2] His great-aunt, Sarah Brenane, sent him to boarding schools in England and France, but he ran away several times. He also injured his left eye in an accident and was left with limited vision and an unsightly appearance—one eye was clouded over and the other enlarged and bulging. When his aunt suffered a reversal of fortunes, he was sent alone to Cincinnati.

Hearn lived on the streets in the Queen City, but eventually he made an acquaintance that proved invaluable. An older man,

FIGURE 14.1 Lafcadio Hearn. *From the Collection of the Public Library of Cincinnati and Hamilton County*

an English printer by the name of Henry Watkin, befriended the short, swarthy, practically blind young man, giving him a place to sleep atop a pile of paper shavings in the back of his print shop and helping him find odd jobs. Over a period of several years, he worked for a commercial newspaper called the *Trade List;* for the Robert Clarke Company as a proofreader and typesetter; as private secretary for Thomas Vickers, the librarian of Cincinnati's public library; and in several other short-lived positions.[3]

Despite his rocky start, Hearn aspired to be a writer, and one day he walked into the office of one of the area's largest newspapers, the *Enquirer,* and shyly approached John Cockerill, managing editor. "When admitted, in a soft, shrinking voice he asked if I ever paid for outside contributions," Cockerill recalled. "I informed him that I was somewhat restricted in the matter of expenditures, but that I would give consideration to what he had to offer." Hearn pulled a manuscript from under his coat, laid it with trepidation on the table, and shrank away.

Cockerill read the manuscript, a review of the latest portion of Alfred, Lord Tennyson's *Idylls of the King,* and was "astonished to find it charmingly written."[4] In early 1872, he published "London Sights," Hearn's first piece.[5]

Hearn worked for the *Enquirer* on a freelance basis for about two years and was on staff and showing great promise by 1874. According to Cockerill, the young man sat in a corner and turned out twelve to fifteen beautifully written columns at a time for a single issue of the newspaper. That was no small feat, given that his vision was so limited he had to rest his eyes "as close to the paper as his nose would permit."[6]

Despite his poor eyesight, Hearn was beginning to use by natural instinct the writing technique that prompted contemporary author Tom Wolfe to include him in his groundbreaking book *The New Journalism.* Along with James Boswell (*The Life of Samuel Johnson*), Charles Dickens (*Sketches by Boz*), Mark Twain (*The Innocents Abroad*), and several others, Hearn is cited by Wolfe as a link in the tradition of what is now called creative nonfiction, or literary journalism. He made nonfiction come alive by creating scenes, using distinctive, highly descriptive details, and incorporating dialogue to establish character.[7] "For me," Hearn once wrote, "words have colour, form, character: they have faces, ports, manners, gesticulations;—they have moods, humours, eccentricities:—they have tints, tones, personalities."[8]

Hearn was also a front-runner in what is now called "immersion journalism," the practice of immersing oneself in the conditions of a story to provide a more personal and realistic account. He drank cattle blood from slaughterhouses to try out a local practice believed to improve health. He disguised himself as a woman to listen to someone purporting to be an "escaped nun." And he ascended the steeple of St. Peter in Chains Cathedral on the back of a steeplejack to write about the view, describing what he managed to see despite his limited vision.[9]

Hearn was never popular with his newspaper colleagues, who called him "Old Semicolon" because he was such a stickler about punctuation and style.[10] But he did turn out good copy, and after writing impressive articles on some of the city's most famous artists—Henry Farny and Frank Duveneck, for example—he turned to "night stories," tales of life in the seedier sections of town. Cockerill was trying to build circulation in a highly competitive market and was more than happy to print Hearn's sensationalist accounts of debauchery and crime. And, for his part, Hearn was totally comfortable in Bucktown and Rat Row, wandering around with ease and telling readers what he saw.

It was in Cincinnati that Hearn first developed an interest in folklore and different cultures, and he preserved lyrics to many songs rendered by black musicians, dockworkers, and others. Those early interests grew, and when he went to New Orleans later, they resulted in stories on voodoo and ghosts. In Japan, they led to the earliest and, arguably, the best Western interpretations of preindustrial Japanese culture.[11]

Hearn also began doing translations of nineteenth-century French Romantic writers, such as Gautier, Flaubert, and Baudelaire, while he was in Cincinnati. He was so intrigued with the French language and French writers that he became distracted by a new French book at the Mercantile Library one day and missed completely his story assignment, a "mad-dog disturbance." He was forgiven by the editors only because he already turned out such a prodigious amount of copy. After he left the city, his interest in French led him to become one of the most recognized translators of short stories by Guy de Maupassant.[12]

On a different note, he famously described Cincinnati's Tyler Davidson Fountain on downtown's Fountain Square as the "old bronze candlestick!"[13] It's a striking phrase, considering that the bronze and granite allegorical fountain is much beloved by Cincinnati and often considered the spiritual center of the city. (The fountain, by Ferdinand von Miller, is officially titled "The Genius of Water.")

In the summer of 1874, Hearn embarked on a joint venture with the artist Henry Farny, who had returned to Cincinnati from Europe about the same time Hearn arrived in town.[14] Hearn and Farny purchased a local publication and turned it into a *Punch*-like newspaper of satirical prose and illustrations called *Ye Giglampz*. *Ye Giglampz*, which operated out of an office at the northwest corner of Fourth and Race Streets, lasted only nine issues, apparently because the new owners couldn't agree on content.[15] Actually, it's amazing the publication got started at all—the title was Farny's rather tasteless joke comparing Hearn's enlarged right eye and thick eyeglasses to a carriage lantern, or gig lamp.[16]

Hearn still had his job at the *Enquirer* when *Ye Giglampz* folded, and in late 1874 he got what might be considered his big break: a murder case. The Tanyard Murder was probably the most gruesome murder in nineteenth-century Cincinnati, and Hearn spared no gory detail in his coverage of it. In a period of a single week, he elevated his name to star status. Readers hung on every word.[17]

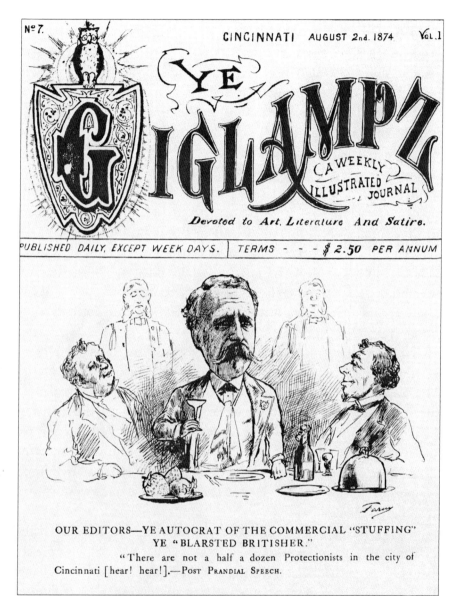

FIGURE 14.2 *Ye Giglampz,* August 2, 1874, edition. *From the Collection of the Public Library of Cincinnati and Hamilton County*

Good times weren't to last, however. After he married a mulatto woman, a freed slave named Alethea "Mattie" Foley, the *Enquirer* fired him for "deplorable moral habits." Interracial marriage was against state miscegenation laws, but the editors may have been pressured by outsiders upset over Hearn's investigative stories. Regardless, his last story appeared in the *Enquirer* on July 9, 1875.[18]

Hearn's marriage didn't last long, and he quickly got a new job, albeit at a reduced salary.[19] He was hired by the *Enquirer*'s competitor, the *Cincinnati Commercial,* and produced for the *Commercial* what are still considered some of the finest descriptions of post–Civil War Negro riverfront life. However, his days in Cincinnati were numbered. In October 1877, after only about a year with the *Commercial,* he decided to leave for New Orleans.[20] Whether he was motivated by a dislike of Cincinnati's weather, remained depressed about his failed marriage, harbored anger at the *Enquirer* for firing him, wanted to see New Orleans, or had some other reason, he was ready to go.

The *Commercial,* not wanting to lose Hearn, asked him to continue as a correspondent, and two of the editors joined Henry Watkin to see him off at the Little Miami train station. He posted his first stories from Memphis while he waited to catch the steamboat *Thompson Dean* and sent others over a period of four or five months after he reached New Orleans. He wrote under the name Ozias Midwinter, a pen name he drew from Wilkie Collins's novel *Armadale.* Ozias was the assumed name of a cursed young man who hated his real name.[21]

Hearn stayed in contact with few Cincinnatians after he left the city, but at least two relationships did survive. One was with Henry Watkin, whom he called "Dad" or "Old Man." Watkin's nickname for Hearn was "the Raven," a reference to Edgar Allan Poe's famous poem and Hearn's gloomy disposition. Hearn considered Poe a major influence and signed notes to Watkin in Cincinnati with drawings of ravens.[22] He continued using the signature in postcards and letters after he left. Watkin saved the correspondence and eventually published it.[23]

It appears that Hearn and Watkin saw each other only once after Hearn's Cincinnati days, although Hearn's letters indicate he hoped for other visits. In June 1887, he came through the city en route to New York and spent a full day talking with Watkin in his print shop on Longworth Street. In a letter written afterward, he expressed his deep love and gratitude to "Dad," signing the letter "affectionately, your son." The two maintained periodic contact through most of Watkin's life.[24]

Hearn also stayed in touch with Henry E. Krehbiel, music critic for the *Cincinnati Gazette* and later music editor of the *New York Tribune* and music critic for *Scribner's Magazine*. Hearn dedicated one of his books to Krehbiel, and Krehbiel later published some of Hearn's correspondence.

Hearn spent about ten years in New Orleans, capturing the colorful character of the city for both local and national publications. He also published several books there, including collections of ghost stories, Creole recipes, proverbs, and *Chita: A Memory of Last Island,* an account of a famous hurricane. In 1887, *Harper's Weekly* sent him on a two-month assignment to the West Indies, and he liked it so much he decided to move there. He spent two years living on Martinique and wrote several more books.

Harper's sent him to Japan in 1890, and he never left. By the time he died in 1904 at the age of fifty-four, he had become a Japanese citizen, assumed a Japanese name, adopted Buddhism, written a dozen books about Japanese culture, married a Japanese woman, fathered four children, and taught extensively, including at Tokyo Imperial University. Widely acclaimed as the man who captured, interpreted, and preserved nineteenth-century Japanese culture for the English-speaking world, he is beloved by the Japanese people to this day. His book of translated Japanese legends, *Kwaidan: Stories and Studies of Strange Things,* was made into a movie in 1965. His house and a Hearn museum in Matsue are popular tourist attractions.

Japan celebrated the hundredth anniversary of Hearn's death with a nine-day, four-city symposium on his work, but he has also been recognized in significant ways in New Orleans, where his home is listed on the National Register of Historic Places. He has even been honored in Ireland, where he summered with his aunt.[25]

Hearn has generally been more celebrated elsewhere than in Cincinnati, but in 1944, the Public Library of Cincinnati and Hamilton County acquired from Henry Farny's son copies of the first eight issues of *Ye Giglampz*, which the elder Farny had purchased from a bookseller when he recognized Hearn's handwriting on them. In 1953, the library added the ninth issue, and thus now has the only complete set known to be in existence.[26] In 1983, the library printed a facsimile of the set, and in 2000, for the 150th anniversary of Hearn's birth, held a major Hearn exhibit.[27] The library has also acquired a collection of Hearniana that once belonged to Thomas Vickers, Hearn's old boss at the library, and other documents from his Japanese family. The library's collection, one of the largest anywhere, includes more than six hundred books and papers.

Cincinnati-based scholarship on Hearn is also growing. University of Cincinnati professor Jon Hughes has edited several collections of Hearn's local articles, lectured about him, and written both a book and a radio play about the Tanyard Murder. The swarthy young man with the pearl eye is once again becoming known in the city where his writing career began.

CHAPTER FIFTEEN

A GOOD ONE

There was a time when Fannie Hurst was one of the highest-paid writers in the country and perhaps the single highest-paid short story writer in the world. The glamorous Miss Hurst, who lived in a Gothic New York triplex with her Yorkshire terriers, socialized with the best-known people in the land: Franklin and Eleanor Roosevelt, Charles and Anne Morrow Lindbergh, Mary Pickford, and many others. Although seldom read today, she authored some thirty books as well as scores of shorter pieces of fiction. Two dozen of her titles were made into films, starring the likes of Gloria Swanson, Frank Sinatra, Claudette Colbert, and Doris Day. Edward R. Murrow interviewed her on *Person to Person*.

Cincinnatians celebrated Fannie Hurst with the rest of the world, but they knew her differently: she was one of their own. Fannie, or Fanye as she was called in her early years, was born on October 19, 1885, in the same bed in which her mother had been born in nearby Hamilton, Ohio. She spent her childhood summers in Hamilton, visiting her relatives and going to Cincinnati's stockyards on business with her grandfather.[1] Although raised in St. Louis, she felt at home in Hamilton (her "summer palace," as she called it), and the area influenced her writing.[2] For example, the first section of one of her best-known books, *Back Street,* is set in the Queen City. It begins: "One evening in one of those Over-the-Rhine cafes which were plentiful along Vine Street of the Cincinnati of the nineties . . ."[3]

FIGURE 15.1   Fannie Hurst. *Washington University and Robert D. Farber University Archives and Special Collections Department, Brandeis University*

Fannie's mother, Rose Koppel, met Samuel Hurst, a German Jew like herself, on a visit to rich relatives in St. Louis. The couple wed on January 11, 1885, at Rose's parents' house on Hamilton's Central Avenue and immediately left for St. Louis, where Sam and his brother had started a canning business. Nine months and ten days later, Rose came home to Hamilton to deliver Fannie in the comfort of familiar surroundings. Afterward, she returned to her husband in St. Louis, but the ritual had begun. Every spring, she and Fannie arrived in Hamilton by train as soon as school was out and stayed for the summer. (Rose's second child died at the age of four, when Fannie was five.[4])

Fannie describes her Hamilton life in detail in her autobiography, *Anatomy of Me: A Wonderer in Search of Herself* (1958). She admits to being a "rather spoiled, overweight brat of a child," but obviously adored her time in her mother's hometown, surrounded by her grandparents, four uncles, and two aunts.[5] Aunt Bettie never married and took over the management of the household when Grandma died, and Aunt Jennie insisted on living there, despite the fact that her husband, Uncle Joe, had to commute to Cincinnati to work. When Rose and Fannie arrived each year, Grandpa pulled a "shabby old basket-phaeton" up to the curb at the train station, and the whole family came inside to greet them. "I can taste and smell Hamilton," Fannie wrote. "We were bourgeois through and through and the bourgeois in me must have responded. . . . I felt at home there."

Fannie struggled with weight issues most of her life and even wrote a book entitled *No Food with My Meals,* but one of the blessings of Hamilton was that she didn't have to worry about anything, even being fat. Grandpa showed her off to his friends and neighbors and went so far as to brag about her size. "She's a good one?" he'd ask the neighbors in his broken English with a German accent. "How much you think she weighs? She's a good one, not?"

Yes, she said, "I was a good one, in Hamilton."

She also found that she could have all the pets she wanted in Hamilton—dogs, goats, rabbits, ponies—and could freely explore the joys of nature, roaming the meadows and pastures and walking along the streams. "The long afternoons of wandering alone stored themselves in my mind," she said. Much later, long after her grandparents had died, the farm was sold, and Fannie always wished she'd bought it. "Hamilton memories are stamped into me as firmly as Grandpa used to mash down tobacco into his smelly old pipe," she said. "I am glad that, despite the vulgarities and petty violence of my background, a modicum of the magnesium of Ohio soil is built into me."

What were the "vulgarities and petty violence" of her background? Her younger sister's death from diphtheria was a life-changing event for the entire family, but there were other problems as well. She loved and admired her father, but never felt close to him. His presence was so stiff it even put a damper on the Koppel fun when he came to collect his family in Hamilton at the end of the summer. He also had financial problems that required the family to move around quite a bit in St. Louis when Fannie was young. The Hursts were forced to live in a boardinghouse for a while.[6]

Fannie was closer to her mother than to her father, but the volatile and controlling Rose wasn't easy either. "When Mama walked into a room filled with ladies," Fannie said, "she doused them like so many candles blown out on a birthday cake."[7]

Still, Fannie was cared for well, was lavished with attention, and felt secure enough that she developed an irrepressible quality. She started writing in high school and published her first work in the student newspaper. Later, she claimed to have submitted stories to the *Saturday Evening Post* from the age of fourteen. After entering college at Washington University, she succeeded in getting a story into a local literary magazine with a national reputation. After graduation in 1909, she floundered a bit, but soon made her way to New York, where she told her parents she was attending Columbia

University. Whether she actually did can't be confirmed, but in January 1912 she did publish her first New York story.[8]

Fannie got her share of rejection letters, but she persevered, and her career leapfrogged once it got started. Her fictional pieces became a staple of the *Saturday Evening Post, Cosmopolitan, Collier's, Harper's Bazaar, Good Housekeeping,* and other national publications. At least one story, "Hochenheimer of Cincinnati," had a Cincinnati theme.

Hurst's first short-story collection, *Just around the Corner,* was published in 1914, and four years later one of her stories, "Her Great Chance," was adapted for film. She published her first novel in 1921 and was on her way to a major writing career. In addition to *Back Street,* her best-known works are the short story "Humoresque" and the novels *Star-Dust: The Story of an American Girl, Lummox,* and *Imitation of Life,* all of which were made into films. She also had a successful radio and television career: she was host of *The Fannie Hurst Showcase* in New York and another popular television show called *Pleased to Meet You.*[9]

Fannie Hurst was best known for what might be called "sob sister" stories, but, despite the negative connotation of that, she had a real feel for the shopgirls, immigrants, and boardinghouse residents trying to scratch out a living in America before World War II. She often came into contact with hardworking and sometimes down-on-their luck types in New York, and observed them in St. Louis and Hamilton and among what she referred to as the "sauerkraut eaters of Cincinnati." Impressively, she developed her writing skills by becoming, as did Lafcadio Hearn, an early practitioner of immersion journalism. Among her efforts to make her stories more realistic were a stay in a New York settlement house, visits to night court, and a stint working in a shoe plant to get to know the young female employees. She claimed to have lived in a tenement and to have worked in a department store too, but those accounts are unverified. (She was known for taking considerable liberties with the truth; she once admitted she had lied about her age so often she couldn't remember how old she was.[10])

Of course, *Back Street* is one of the most interesting stories for Cincinnatians. First published in serialized form as "Back Streets" in *Cosmopolitan,* it subsequently came out as a novel and later was adapted not once but three times for film.[11] It features a woman named Ray (named for one of Fannie's aunts), who lives with her father on Baymiller Street in Cincinnati. The first 130 pages of *Back Street,* through book 1, are laden with well-known local names of the period: Pogue's department store, the Stag and Alms hotels, Wielert's Saloon, and Rathman's Steamboat Company, along with many other places still in existence today: Plum Street Temple, Mecklenburg's Garden, the Cincinnati Zoo, Colerain Avenue, and Eden Park. The town of Hamilton also receives prominent mention.

The *Cincinnati Enquirer* panned *Back Street,* even though it reached number eight on the best-seller list. An unattributed review dated January 31, 1931, complained that, while Miss Hurst used *Enquirer* files for her research and her book featured many local sites, "atmosphere and color are lacking." According to the reviewer, *Back Street* improved only after Ray left Cincinnati and Hurst gave up all attempts to capture the "rhythm of the old city through a recital of names, dates and places."[12]

One assumption that has often been made about *Back Street* isn't true. During a 1965 visit to speak at a luncheon in honor of the Salvation Army's eighty years in the city (she was a member of the national Salvation Army's executive committee), she was taken on a tour of Over-the-Rhine and expressed pleasure that the area was "so descriptive" of what she had in mind when she wrote the book. However, she was surprised when she learned that there really was a Back Street; she said she gave the story its name simply because it fit the theme. (There is also a real Baymiller Street, in the city's West End, but if she commented on that, it is not reported.)

During her Over-the-Rhine tour, Fannie recalled fond memories of the city: a trip on the riverboat *Island Queen,* visits to the "lovely"

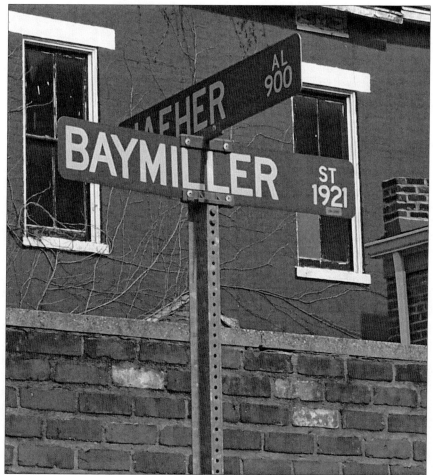

FIGURE 15.2 Cincinnati's Baymiller Street, 2010. *Photograph by Louis E. Enzweiler*

Cincinnati Zoo, and "eating delicious cottage cheese with green things [chives] in it." She also mentioned the tradition of music in the city, St. Peter in Chains Cathedral, Isaac M. Wise Temple, and City Hall. She complimented Cincinnati on keeping its old land-marks and sustaining a "culture as old as any in the country."

When Fannie arrived in Cincinnati for the 1965 visit, she brought her Yorkshire terrier, Lilliputian, with her. "We've learned all the sneaky techniques" necessary to avoid the baggage compartment, she said. She kept the tiny dog, which weighed less than two pounds, in her pocket, under her sleeve, or covered with a scarf. "What dog?" she once asked a conductor who challenged her. "That one," the man said, pointing to Lilliputian. "That? That's a mammal," she said.[13]

Fannie Hurst visited the greater Cincinnati area several other times as a celebrity. The local press reported a September 1928 visit with her mother to see her Aunt Jennie and Uncle William Frieder, a vice president of a Cincinnati bank, who by then lived at the Alms.[14] She also came through town in October 1932 during a vacation trip to the West. (She called such trips "vagabonding.") During that visit, she was interviewed at the Netherland Plaza Hotel (now the Hilton Cincinnati Netherland Plaza) on her views about women. "I would rather be a woman in this generation than in any other age," she told the reporter. She thought women were doing a wonderful job working both inside and outside the home and urged them to develop an interest in government as the next step.[15]

Fannie visited Hamilton in 1955 for the Hamilton Jewish Tercentenary and in 1966 as guest of honor for "Fannie Hurst Days." During the first of those visits, she spoke to high school students at assemblies, appeared at a public library, and visited her birth site on Central Avenue, by then a lumberyard. She mentioned to interviewers that she planned to write a new book using the Cincinnati area as background and a Cincinnati newspaperman as hero.[16] (The plans never came to fruition.) She also described her writing habits to a reporter: at seventy, she still rose at 5:30 a.m., walked for an hour and a half, and then worked five or six hours. "I try to write without the white sauce," she said. "I like clarity. I write with great anguish."[17]

As she gained fame, Fannie Hurst stepped more and more into the role of social activist, using her celebrity to focus on such issues as race relations, women's rights, public health, and humane treatment for animals. She took up the causes of women, African Americans, homosexuals, and other minority groups before that kind of crusading became popular. She is often recognized for mentoring the African American writer Zora Neale Hurston.

Fannie was appointed to several national commissions, including one on housing and one on workers' compensation. She also served as a U.S. delegate to the World Health Organization in Geneva in 1932, promoted Liberty Bonds, raised money to help refugees from Nazi Germany, and rallied support in the 1950s for the new nation of Israel.[18]

And then there was her unusual marriage. She married Jacques S. Danielson, a talented pianist, in 1915, but they decided to keep the marriage a secret. They finally announced it on their fifth anniversary in a lengthy *New York Times* article in which Fannie explained that they had decided "to sail into the sea of matrimony on a bark of their own designing." They were determined to make sure they maintained their individuality and their ability to work successfully and wanted to keep their marriage fresh by avoiding what most marriages became: "sordid endurance tests." They maintained different schedules and different housing and "met by inclination, not duty." "We decided that seven breakfasts a week opposite to one another might prove irksome," she said. "Our average is two."[19] They were still married at the time of Jack's death in 1952.

With her striking appearance and dramatic manner, Fannie Hurst became a sort of cultural icon. She had pitch-black hair, white skin, and bright red lips, and wore clothing and jewelry with flair. Her signature was a large enamel calla lily set in diamonds and topaz, which she variously explained as standing for peace and serenity, individuality, or her husband's love.[20] When she died in New York in 1968 at the age of eighty-two, the *New York Times* published a front-page obituary.[21] F. Scott Fitzgerald had once described her as a writer who didn't produce a single tale "that would last ten years," but he wasn't entirely correct. Many of the films made from her stories are still highly regarded, and the Jewish girl from Hamilton is still considered one of the twentieth century's most colorful characters. With her extraordinary storytelling and her exceptional ability to advocate for the poor and the neglected, she had a unique voice. As one writer recently pointed out, she is finally beginning to attract the interest of scholars of American literature and Jewish American culture, and her work "is ripe for rediscovery by feminist cultural historians."[22]

CHAPTER SIXTEEN

HERETIC AT CINCINNATI

T he poet and the rabbi didn't look alike, and those who knew them say their personalities weren't at all similar, but there's a striking similarity to their photos even so, something beyond white hair and time-lined faces. It's something about the eyes, a spiritual quality.

Four-time Pulitzer Prize winner Robert Frost and Dr. Victor Reichert, rabbi of Cincinnati's Rockdale Temple, were friends. Their friendship was so important and so lasting that it influenced both their lives and their work and became a subject for Frost biographies. It also became the central thread in a little-known, decade-long connection between Frost and the city of Cincinnati.

Frost was predisposed to like it in the Queen City: one of his earliest memories was going to the train station in Oakland, California, to see his father off to Cincinnati, where he was to serve as a delegate to the 1880 Democratic National Convention. Will Frost was all dressed up in a top hat and frock coat, and a brass band played.[1] It was a big occasion, and his son never forgot it. In January 1922, when the Ohio Valley Poetry Society invited him to speak at the Literary Club rooms on Eighth Street, he readily accepted.

Frost had not yet received any Pulitzer Prizes or made his memorable appearance at President Kennedy's inauguration. But he was already celebrated, and Cincinnati gave him an enthusiastic welcome. According to the *Cincinnati Enquirer,* he spoke on "Is Poetry Highbrow or Lowbrow?" and got three encores for poetry recitations. The audience "was as huge as it was enthusiastic, the motors of the members blocking the streets in all directions."[2]

However, it was his next visit, one of more than a half dozen he made to Cincinnati, that proved most significant. That was when he met Rabbi Reichert.

In the fall of 1938, Louise Reichert heard that Robert Frost was coming to town to speak under the auspices of *Talaria,* a now-defunct Cincinnati poetry magazine. *Talaria* editors Annette Patton Cornell and B. Y. Williams had worked for weeks to raise three hundred dollars to sponsor "Robert Frost in recital." Tickets were on sale for a dollar fifty each, a sum considered exorbitant at the time. Mrs. Reichert insisted she and her husband attend because she had heard Frost speak when she was a student at Smith College. She had loved him, and her eyes still sparkled many years later when she described the impact he'd had on the Smith College women during his appearance at a bookstore in North Hampton in 1926. "He was so handsome; all of us fell in love with him. He had sex appeal . . . a wonderful speaking voice . . . he was brilliant . . . he gave a dramatic reading . . . he had a tremendous charm. How could you not like him?"[3]

Her husband, however, said, "No thanks." Rabbi Reichert was a poet and writer himself, and, before coming to Cincinnati to study at Hebrew Union College, he had earned a graduate degree from the Columbia University School of Journalism. He eventually published a collection of poetry called *Tower of David,* and he already had a favorite poet, Edwin Arlington Robinson. He didn't need another.

The charming Louise prevailed, however, and when Frost stood at the podium in front of four hundred people gathered in the ballroom of the Gibson Hotel (near Fountain Square where the Westin now stands), Reichert sat in the front row so he could study the speaker. As the speech wore on, however, he noticed that Frost was actually studying him. When it was over, he and his wife joined a group surrounding the poet, and Reichert realized he had been sized up. "I know all about you," Frost said without preamble. "Why don't you come up to Vermont?"[4]

Frost had just bought the Homer Noble Farm in Ripton, Vermont, and was planning to spend his summers there, writing poetry and teaching at the Bread Loaf Writers' Conference, a summer writing program he had helped popularize. At sixty-four, he was still handsome, with pale blue eyes and a memorable resonant speaking voice, and he could be quite genial, often chatting for hours with students or other fans who liked to hear him talk. However, he could also be temperamental and self-absorbed, especially at that time, when he was grieving the recent death of his wife, Elinor.[5]

Reichert was more than twenty years younger than Frost and a family man with two sons. He had an infectious grin, a square jaw, and an intelligent look, and was taller than the poet, who grew more stooped and shorter as he got older. To the extent that Frost was self-absorbed, Reichert was just the opposite—warm, kind, and outgoing, according to those who knew him.

It wasn't until several years later, after World War II, that Reichert finally boarded a train to Vermont to accept Frost's invitation. In Ripton, the two men took the first of many rambling walks through the woods of the Green Mountains and stayed up late discussing the Bible. Reichert was a dedicated biblical scholar who developed a reputation as an eminent theologian, publishing a commentary on the books of the Bible that went through at least ten printings. Frost was an original thinker with an excellent memory. The two were well matched and relished their intellectual talks.

They also played tennis, which they both enjoyed, even though the matches were difficult. Mrs. Reichert recalled in a 2003 interview that Frost was extremely competitive and "had to win." "Every Fourth of July, Frost invited the Bread Loaf faculty and students to have a baseball game. On one occasion, Hewitt Joyce, head of the English Department at Dartmouth and acting head of Bread Loaf, caught Frost's ball, which would have been a home run. This was the sweetest, most elegant man," Mrs. Reichert said. "Frost never had much to do with him after that."

The Reicherts loved the lush, wooded paths and the mountain peaks in Vermont, and soon they were going to Ripton every summer. Of course, as Mrs. Reichert pointed out, the main attraction was Frost, always Frost. For the first few seasons, the Reicherts stayed at Bread Loaf, and then, in 1945, they bought a summer place of their own, a hundred-year-old converted school known as the "Schoolhouse."

The Schoolhouse was only two miles from the Homer Noble Farm, and Frost and the Reicherts saw each other often. Sometimes the Cincinnati couple took Frost out to dinner, and afterward they'd drop him off in the dark, lending him a flashlight ("He never had one," Mrs. Reichert said) to help him navigate the last quarter mile of his long dirt driveway, which took him past a farmhouse and through a grove of trees to the modest wooden cabin where he lived. Frost wrote many of his poems in that cabin, sitting in a Morris chair with a board in his lap as a makeshift writing table.

One day Frost telephoned Reichert to say he had something he wanted him to hear. Reichert told him to come on over, and the two men sat on the porch of the Schoolhouse while Frost read a draft of *A Masque of Reason,* a one-act play in verse about the biblical character Job. Reichert, who had studied Job for years, listened carefully and was "overwhelmed." He expressed his admiration and made several comments, and the poem was published not long afterward. When he saw it in print, Reichert was gratified to find that Frost had used one of his own lines, "Here endeth chapter forty-three of Job," to close it.[6]

The friendship of the two men thrived in the Vermont summers, and the Reicherts became an integral part of the community there. Reichert taught for a while at the Bread Loaf School of English and also initiated a popular annual sermon on a selected book of the Bible at the nearby Community Methodist Church. He was eventually listed as the church's "resident rabbi."

But the friendship grew in Cincinnati as well. In April 1944, Frost returned to the city to speak at the University of Cincinnati under the auspices of the Charles Phelps Taft Memorial Fund.[7] According to an unpublished journal kept by then–University of Cincinnati president Raymond Walters, the poet spoke to eight hundred people in Wilson Hall on April 19. He "looked tired and wan after his recovery from pneumonia in Florida this winter. But his spirit was joyous, as ever."[8]

Naturally, Reichert, who taught a course at the University of Cincinnati called Journalism and the Bible as Literature, urged his students to attend Frost's lecture. Luella LeVee, a Rockville, Maryland, author who was then a nineteen-year-old coed, recalled Reichert in a telephone interview as "an outgoing man" who took a lot of time with young people. When he recommended the Frost lecture, she went.

It was wartime, and the audience of students, dressed in sloppy joe shirts and bobby socks, was generously sprinkled with boys in uniform. While Frost gave a speech on "The Claim for Poetry" in Wilson Hall, Miss LeVee, a petite, dark-haired young woman, took out a pad and started to sketch.

Frost's face was lined with age, and he looked uncomfortable in a dark suit with a stiff-collared shirt, but he still had the dramatic flair his biographers mention. His voice rose, Miss LeVee said, and faded, paused and roared back, with a shake of his head or an emphatic gesture. But, even while he spoke, he glanced with amusement at the pretty sophomore sketching his likeness in front of him.

After the lecture, Frost was ushered away to sign copies of the book that had earned him a Pulitzer Prize the year before, *A Witness Tree*, which includes such familiar lines as:

> I could give all to Time except—except
> What I myself have held. But why declare
> The things forbidden that while the Customs slept

I have crossed to Safety with? For I am There,
And what I would not part with I have kept.

Miss LeVee waited her turn for an autograph, but instead of offering him a book to sign, she handed him her sketch. "Stick around, and we'll talk," he told her, signing his name and handing back the sketch.

And so they did: the seventy-year-old literary lion and the nineteen-year-old Cincinnati student, facing each other in straight-backed chairs in a bare classroom. A jug of forsythia sat on the windowsill, and songs of the air corps boys wafted through the open window. Luella took out some of her writing and gave it to Frost. He began reading one of her poems out loud, intoning the words as he had his own moments earlier.

"It's not real—it doesn't ring true," she exclaimed in embarrassment.

Frost was kind. He praised her newspaper stories and gave her several pieces of advice: read the good writers and the good poets and "then have the courage to be new. And don't plan the writing," he said. "Just write. What you don't need is to stick around this school." After all, he himself had simply taken up poetry in high school and dropped out of Harvard and Dartmouth. "But," he added, "don't tell anybody I told you to do it, because I'm here under the auspices of the university."

Miss LeVee took Frost's advice, as she'd taken Reichert's. Shortly afterward she dropped out of school and started earning her living by writing. Only years later did she tell anyone what Frost had advised. And then she went back to school and got a degree at Northern Kentucky University.[9]

Two years after his appearance at Wilson Hall, Frost returned to the city, once again lecturing for the Taft Fund at the University of Cincinnati.[10] The Reicherts gave a dinner party for him, and after it was over Frost sat down in his favorite wing chair in the living room to chat with the couple. The rabbi mentioned that he had to preach the next morning for the First Day of Succoth, the Feast of the Tabernacles. Frost said he had once preached in a friend's church.

"You never preached for me," Reichert said.

"You never asked me," Frost replied.

"I'm asking you now."[11]

That settled it. Frost got up to return to his hotel to prepare for the morning service. But before he left, he asked Mrs. Reichert to provide provisions for his now-famous breakfast, two raw eggs, which he put in his briefcase. "He coddled them in hot water," she said. "I asked him why he didn't just call room service, but no . . ."

It was 10 p.m. by then, so there was little time to alert the congregation, but Reichert did what he could to inform his flock that there would be a guest speaker the next morning.

"I have come here as a sort of exchange preacher with Rabbi Reichert," Frost began the next day at Rockdale, a large Romanesque building in Avondale that has since been demolished. He came, he said, not just out of friendship, but out of "affection." Then he gave his sermon, using as his starting point a reading the rabbi had just done from the *Union Prayerbook*. In a now-often-quoted line, he defined religion as "a straining of the spirit forward to a wisdom beyond wisdom."[12]

Over the years there have been many scholarly debates about Frost's spiritual beliefs, and he is often considered an atheist. But in the eloquent Rockdale sermon, he seemed clear enough about his faith. He called irreligion "worse than atheism" and advocated faith as a necessity. Reichert was so convinced Frost was a believer that he later defended him in a paper called "What, That Atheist," which he wrote for Cincinnati's Literary Club in the 1980s. "There is not the slightest doubt in my mind about the deep, deep religious nature of Robert Frost," he said.[13]

That sermon in Cincinnati also proved significant for a literary reason. As Frost developed his message for it, he hit upon a suitable ending for *A Masque of Mercy,* a dramatic poem with which he had been struggling. He soon completed the poem and sent it off to his publisher.[14]

Frost made other visits to Cincinnati in the late 1940s and early 1950s, and he always saw his friends when he was there. In November 1954, at the age of eighty, he returned to receive an honorary doctor of laws degree at the University of Cincinnati. When he hopped off the train at Cincinnati's Winton Place station, his eyes sparkled and he had a springy step, even though he had just recovered from a wrenched knee. "I went down two stairs when I thought I was taking one a couple of Saturdays ago," he said to the men who awaited him. "But I didn't feel too badly about it. There are lots of wrenched knees on these football Saturdays."[15]

The men who met Frost's train that day were Reichert and Dr. William S. Clark II, then head of the University of Cincinnati's English Department and a former student of Frost's. Frost knew Clark well and sometimes stayed at his home. That time, however, he was slated to stay with the Reicherts, in their first-floor guest room on Rose Bud Avenue.

That evening Frost borrowed a copy of his own collected works from Reichert's son David, and he and the Reichert family drove to campus. At 8:30, Dr. Walters, president of the university, presented Frost with an honorary degree, and the audience of twelve hundred rose in a spontaneous ovation. Frost was pleased. He held no college degree of his own, but he loved honorary degrees and ultimately accumulated a total of forty-four. He later had the degree hoods made into quilts. The University of Cincinnati's, his twenty-seventh, is part of a quilt on display at the University of New Hampshire library.

After the awards ceremony, Frost, his mane of white hair shining under a black mortarboard and a patterned tie peeping from the neckline of his velvet-trimmed academic robe, gave a lecture and read from David's copy of his collected poems.[16] Then he and various invited guests went back to the Reicherts' for an informal gathering.

"The first time he was here," Mrs. Reichert said, "we had a reception for him, but he didn't like it. He didn't like shaking hands with a lot of people." The party went on late into the night, and when Mrs. Reichert got up the next morning she was still exhausted. But Frost was already up and fully dressed, sitting in the living room. "Are we having a big family breakfast?" he asked.

David Reichert, the couple's oldest son, who became a Cincinnati lawyer, remembered the visits and liked Frost. He was "a very warm person. I never saw any of the dark side" sometimes mentioned in biographies. Frost had a difficult life that included a son's suicide, a daughter's mental illness, and other traumatic events, and he could be both contrary and full of rage at times. But David, then a teenager, saw none of that. Frost had broad interests, he said, and the two of them had lively discussions, including one he remembered about the boxer Joe Louis. He also recalled the more elevated, philosophical discussions between his father and Frost. "They enjoyed bantering back and forth. I didn't appreciate it at the time." When David Reichert married a few years later, he took his new bride to Ripton for a delayed honeymoon. Their celebration included a dinner with Robert Frost.[17]

The same year Frost received the University of Cincinnati degree, he gave two lectures as part of the university's Elliston Lecture Series and attended a reading of *A Masque of Reason* by the Cincinnati MacDowell Society. The latter performance was prefaced by "A Few Words about the Book of Job" by Rabbi Reichert.[18] When Frost left the Reicherts' home that time, he left behind one of his books, inscribed "To Victor, for supporting me through the presentation of my heresies at Cincinnati, November 21, '54 RF."[19]

In 1960, Reichert sponsored Frost to receive an honorary Doctor of Humane Letters degree at Hebrew Union College. That he held honorary degrees from two schools, the University of Cincinnati and Hebrew Union, only a stone's throw apart amused the

FIGURE 16.1 Robert Frost with Rabbi Victor Reichert (*right*) at Hebrew Union College, 1960. *Photograph by Jack Warner Studios, The Marcus Center of the American Jewish Archives*

poet. "Now," Frost quipped, "I can walk down both sides of Clifton Avenue and feel at home."[20]

During that stay Frost was invited to be Reichert's guest for a visit to the Literary Club. Before the evening meeting, Reichert hosted a dinner party for six people at the Bankers Club, where Frost, then eighty-six, "had two martinis and was still able to listen attentively to the paper of the evening." Afterward, in his remarks to the club, he cited a favorite couplet from his poem "A Concept Self-Conceived": "Forgive, O Lord, my little jokes on Thee / And I shall forgive your great big joke on me!"

He also pointed out the difference between his host, Rabbi Reichert, and St. Jerome. Jerome, he said, studied the Old Testament to show how much we need the New; Reichert studied the Old Testament to prove you can get along without the New.

In the club's guest book, Frost wrote, "I dared not be radical when young / For fear of becoming conservative when old."[21]

That was Frost's last visit to Cincinnati, but it wasn't the last time the Reicherts saw him. They met for the last time just after Frost came back from his much-publicized trip to Russia to see Nikita Khrushchev. Frost sat on the Reicherts' love seat at the Schoolhouse in Vermont. "What do you think are the chances of life after death?" Frost asked. But the rabbi turned the question back to him. "What do *you* think?" he said.

Frost thought for a moment. "With so many ladders going up everywhere," he finally said, "there must be something for them to lean against." That was the fall of 1962. He died the following January.

Reichert lived twenty-seven years after Frost's death, dying in 1990 at the age of ninety-three. After his retirement at sixty-five, he stayed busy teaching, writing, and preaching and often gave talks on or wrote about his friendship with Robert Frost. He also shared his memories with a Vermont friend, Andrew R. Marks, who published a small book in 1994 entitled *The Rabbi and The Poet,* focused on the Vermont life the pair shared. The two men came from different backgrounds, Reichert told Marks. On one hand, the poet had "several hundred years of America on his side," while the rabbi was "first generation American with several generations of tailors, horse thieves, ex-convicts and rabbis from Poland and Germany."[22]

But they also had a lot in common. You could see it in their eyes.

CHAPTER SEVENTEEN

BABBITTRY

Was it Cincinnati? Or Minneapolis, Milwaukee, or Kansas City? Or perhaps some other midsized American city? Those questions have swirled for decades around Sinclair Lewis's best-selling 1920s satire *Babbitt* and the fictional city in which it is set. Fortunately, scholars are now in agreement: the answer is "yes." Not one, but a number of cities influenced Lewis's creation of Zenith. And Cincinnati probably had the largest role.

In February 1921, the thirty-six-year-old Lewis arrived in the Queen City for a several-month stay, fresh from the publication of *Main Street,* the novel with which he was making his name after years of relative obscurity.[1] Ostensibly on a lecture tour for *Main Street,* he was determined to use the tour not just for lecturing, which he didn't enjoy, but to conduct research for his new novel.[2] He had already organized his plot and structure and decided he would focus on a businessman named George Babbitt who lived in a fictional heartland state called Winnemac. But *Babbitt* needed details for a realistic feel. Cincinnati was where he would start gathering them.

Fittingly, "Red" Lewis settled into the Queen City Club, the social club Joseph Longworth and his friends established in 1874. The club was incorporated "for literary purposes and for mutual improvement," but from the beginning it was an elegant private setting where many important business connections were made.[3] Lewis lived in a pied-à-terre in the club's original building, which was located on

FIGURE 17.1 Original Queen City Club building, southwest corner of Seventh and Elm. *Courtesy of the Queen City Club*

the southwest corner of Seventh and Elm in what was once the well-to-do residential neighborhood of the West End. By the time Lewis visited, the area housed a livery stable and a brothel and was crowded with many low-income residents. (The club moved to its current building at Fourth and Broadway in 1927.[4])

Club records from the 1920s make no mention of Lewis, which is not surprising given the limited scope of the records and the club's practice of quiet discretion. Nevertheless, it is not difficult to picture the scene. Lewis would have been well tended in the stately red brick building with its black walnut– and oak-paneled rooms and could easily have met and observed a wide variety of people as they came and went. He could even observe without being observed himself. One letter he wrote from the club mentions "two young-old gentlemen from Kentucky" who were "getting beautifully stewed" with a bottle of liquor and a bowl of ice in the room next door.[5] Soon after his arrival, he wrote to Harcourt, his publisher, sounding pleased: "Bully time, met lots of people, really getting the feeling of life here. Fine for Babbitt."[6]

Lewis would also have been allowed his privacy to read and study the local newspapers and to write up his findings in his notebook, which is now preserved at the Beinecke Rare Book and Manuscript Library of Yale University. One clipping he stuck in his notebook mentions city areas affected by road construction. He annotated it with names of districts where his character Babbitt could hold rental properties. He also saved clippings about a Cincinnati apartment house to help determine accurate real estate costs and read the society columns of the newspaper to gather useful syntax and language. He even jotted down "locutions," expressions and variations that might be useful in his writing.[7]

Most of what Lewis learned in his local research went into creating fictional characters and his fictional city, but he did cite Cincinnati by name in *Babbitt*. The Cincinnati Symphony Orchestra, the city's machine tool industry, and the soap business all receive positive mention. And Babbitt reflects on a motor tour "through Ohio, and the exploration of Cleveland, Cincinnati, and Columbus."[8]

The book also includes detailed references to a Union Club and an Athletic Club, but it isn't clear whether they were drawn from local organizations. Given that he was staying in a similar sort of place, the logical conclusion is that they were.

Lewis lectured at least once while he was in town, under the auspices of the H. & S. Pogue Co. department store. The store took out an ad billing Lewis as "author of 'Main Street'" and announcing that he would speak at three o'clock on the afternoon of Wednesday, March 9, at the store's ninth-floor auditorium. Autographed copies of *Main Street* were to be available for sale.[9] According to the *Cincinnati Post,* several hundred people attended the lecture. It was entitled "Spiritual Specialization," and in it

Lewis took stabs at the evangelist Billy Sunday, who happened to be preaching in town. Sunday, he said, was "an unusually able actor with a gift for vulgarity. He seems to be sincere; no doubt he is sincere. But he loves to talk about 'stinking' things. I don't think pet words of his help the cause of religion."[10]

The *Post* didn't report Lewis's comments on *Main Street* or describe his physical appearance. However, a description of another lecture during the period gives us a mental picture. He is said to have rambled and fidgeted, "buttoning and unbuttoning his coat, picking up and laying down his Ingersoll dollar watch," pacing around the stage, and occasionally consulting his notes.[11]

In May, after visiting several other midwestern cities, Lewis left for England to do the actual writing of *Babbitt,* which was a satire of the conformity and complacency of the 1920s middle class. He published it in 1922. Many years later, detailed maps and plans for the book were discovered in a Vermont farmhouse where he had once lived. They show just how extensively he worked to transform his imagined characters and settings into a realistic story.[12] They also indicate better than any previous evidence that he intended to create a totally unique city, not simply to recreate a single place he had visited. Still, the details he gathered in Cincinnati were helpful, and *Babbitt* is still considered an important book. The words "Babbitt" and "Babbittry," referring to a person or practice of conforming unthinkingly to prevailing middle-class standards, quickly slipped into common usage, and they remain in the dictionary today.

The 1921 visit is perhaps Lewis's most significant connection to Cincinnati, but it is not the only one. In 1933, he returned to the city to do research for his novel *Work of Art,* which uses the hotel industry as a backdrop. He stayed at what was then the Netherland Plaza Hotel and interviewed Robert W. Ryan, the hotel's sales and advertising director. By that time, Lewis had won the first Nobel Prize for Literature ever awarded an American (1930) and was even more famous than during his earlier stay. Nevertheless, according to Ryan, he was quite shy until he started asking questions. After that, "questions simply bubbled from him." *Work of Art* was published in 1934.[13]

Cincinnati is also mentioned in his novel *Arrowsmith* (1925), for which he was awarded a Pulitzer Prize. (He declined the award.)

Lewis visited Cincinnati several other times. He was interviewed by local newspapers in 1938 when he came to speak to the University of Cincinnati's Business and Professional Men's Group. He told the *Cincinnati Post* that he intended to retire at eighty, set himself up as a "one of those sweetly nasty oracles" for three years afterward, then "croak." "That's what I'll do," he said at the Netherland Plaza. "Croak when I'm 83."

"How do you know, Mr. Lewis?" he was asked.

"Well, can you prove I won't?" (Unfortunately, he was wrong. He died January 10, 1951, at the age of sixty-five.)

According to the *Post*, Lewis was "long and gangly, likes to cross his legs as he talks or slouch to a window and peer out." Although he was considered one of the best interpreters of American life, he said he knew less about the United States than anything else. "Maybe that's because I live here and appreciate how much there is to know that I can't possibly retain."[14]

In an interview with the *Cincinnati Enquirer*, he touched upon his views on education and the career of his second wife, journalist Dorothy Thompson, and dismissed questions about his next novel because he wasn't ready to talk about it.[15] In the formal lecture at the University of Cincinnati's College of Medicine auditorium, he presented some of his personal views on current economic and political thought and touched upon "Dale Carnegie-ism, education and advertising." He also said the country needed leadership that offered the "hellfire and damnation of Jonathan Edwards, coupled with the humor of Mark Twain." The *Cincinnati Times-Star* described the talk as "epigram-studded."[16]

Lewis also spoke to a large crowd at the Cincinnati Woman's Club tea room around that time. According to one of the club's printed histories, he made "a few pertinent remarks about the theatre."[17]

In late 1941, it was announced that Lewis would return to the city on a nationwide tour for a debate entitled "Can It Happen Here?" with the noted writer, historian, and University of Cincinnati graduate Dr. Lewis Browne. The Cincinnati Rotary Club took the opportunity to proclaim to Lewis that "all is forgiven." "As I recall, you were not very indulgent of luncheon clubs or civic clubs at the time you wrote your book 'Main Street,'" the chairman of the club's program committee wrote in a publicized invitation. "However, since that time you may have changed your opinion. Nevertheless, in view of this, we are very desirous of having you as our guest to see how the Cincinnati Rotary Club is conducted."[18]

A story in the *Cincinnati Times-Star,* written at the time of Lewis's death, mentions that he was "the guest of the late John G. Kidd at the Rotary Club," so apparently he accepted the club's invitation.[19] And he definitely participated in the scheduled debate, which was held on December 9, 1941, under the auspices of the University of Cincinnati's Contemporary Thought Series. At the university's Wilson Auditorium, Lewis took the negative position on the question of whether fascism could happen in the United States, and Browne took the affirmative. However, at the conclusion of the debate, Browne admitted he had argued academically, and he and Lewis agreed that fascism "can't happen here."[20]

CHAPTER EIGHTEEN

THE POET LAUREATE OF GREETING CARDS

Helen Steiner Rice may not have won her credentials from the Library of Congress, but she is often referred to as a poet laureate—the "poet laureate of greeting cards."[1] And although she wasn't a native Cincinnatian, she lived in the city for fifty years, garnering international fame for her work for a Cincinnati company. A foundation she established continues to benefit the city's underprivileged.

Helen Elaine Steiner showed great promise from the start. Born May 19, 1900, in Lorain, Ohio, on Lake Erie near Cleveland, she grew up reading the Bible and the encyclopedia, absorbing her maternal grandmother's stories, and writing rhyming verses.[2] "On Sunday night we'd have our family worship time," she said. "That was one of the blessings of a radioless, televisionless era: there was time for family conversation. Without fail, I'd climb up on a chair and preach, using all the Bible verses I knew."[3] Small in stature (barely more than five feet tall when full grown), she was a dynamo—attractive, photogenic, outgoing, and always popular.

Helen planned to go to college and study law after high school, but it didn't turn out that way. Shortly after she graduated, her father, a railroad engineer, died in the flu epidemic of 1918. She took a job demonstrating how to make silk lampshades at the Lorain Electric Light and Power Company and became the main support for her mother and younger sister.

With the type of commitment that characterized all her efforts, Helen quickly moved up in the company. She volunteered to

FIGURE 18.1 Helen Steiner Rice. *Cincinnati Museum Center–Cincinnati Historical Society Library*

"trim" office windows and eventually made her way into advertising and sales. It wasn't long before she gained statewide and then national attention by speaking out on behalf of the electric industry and as an advocate for women. One newspaper article quoted her as saying, "Women are tired of being parsley on the platter of business," and another called her "the Sweetheart of the Electrical Industry." *Forbes* magazine awarded her first place in a competition for an article on how to do public relations. She was so prominent at twenty-five that she was included in a group invited to the White House to meet President Calvin Coolidge.[4]

After five years in her job, Helen was recruited to run a public relations bureau for the Cleveland Illuminating Company, but in the spring of 1927 she left to set up her own speaker's bureau. In a brochure she did for her new business, she described herself as "Nationally Known Lecturer, Writer, Humorist, Pep-Talker, After Dinner Speaker, Organizer, Promoter, and Educational Director." And she was successful, commanding impressive fees, garnering regular front-page coverage, and charming everyone she met. Among her fans was a handsome, wealthy young banker who was assigned to shepherd her around when she was invited to speak to the Dayton Rotary Club. The day after Franklin Rice met Helen Steiner, he called off his engagement to another woman, and in less than a week he rolled up in front of her Lorain house in a limousine.[5]

Franklin and Helen were married at New York's Plaza Hotel in early 1929, and she had what she described as a "fairy tale kind of marriage to a beautiful man." She quit her job and moved into his fourteen-room house on Dayton's Grand Avenue, where the two of them assumed the good life, complete with Caribbean vacations, expensive cars, servants, and parties.[6] Unfortunately, it wasn't to last. Franklin lost everything in the 1929 stock market crash and grew increasingly depressed. Helen quickly sprang into action. She reestablished her speaker's bureau and worked as a contract bridge counselor.

It was through an old friend that Helen Steiner Rice met J. P. Gibson, the owner of a Cincinnati greeting card company. When she started her bridge consultancy, she contacted him to purchase playing cards to resell to her bridge customers. She also pitched a promotional idea, almost as an afterthought. Gibson snapped her up for an assignment, and soon she was a Gibson employee, living in Cincinnati. Franklin came to visit on weekends but stayed in the Dayton house, looking for work. He committed suicide in October 1932, less than four years after he married Helen.

Rice, now a widow at thirty-two, resolved to pay off Franklin's debts and threw herself into the marketing job at Gibson. She also began writing greeting cards, and in the mid-1930s was named greeting card editor. Feature stories on her cards and her thoughts on Christmas card trends often appeared in Cincinnati newspapers.[7]

For more than twenty-five years, Helen Steiner Rice wrote mostly humorous verse for Gibson; she described herself as among "the first of the smart alecks" in the greeting card business.[8] However, for her friends and family and for her "verse diary," she wrote inspirational verse, throwing off rhymed inspirational poems for just about any occasion, whether to thank a department store clerk for extra service or as a sympathy note. "My calling," she once said, "seems to be putting old spiritual truths into simple little rhymes. . . . I never rewrite. I don't type. When I think of a poem I just write it down. That's it. No second drafts. No polish. When people ask how they come to me I can't answer." She considered herself a "messenger of the Lord."[9] (She did keep voluminous files of newspaper clippings and copied out excerpts from books by hand to draw upon.[10])

When Helen first came to Cincinnati, she moved into the Netherland Plaza Hotel, the only hotel she knew in the city, but soon, at the suggestion of a friend, she relocated to the top floor of the Gibson Hotel on Walnut Street.[11] The hotel was a few blocks from the seven-story brick Gibson Art Company, situated on the southeast corner of Fourth and Plum. Helen lived and ate most of her meals at the hotel for more than forty years. Her room was her home, and the staff her family. She called the woman who cleaned her room "Mom."[12]

For many years Helen walked to work and to the nearby Wesley Methodist Chapel for church on Sunday. One teenager in the choir later described the fashion statement she made when she arrived with her "beautiful impeccable attire and sincere pretty smile. Everything about Mrs. Rice was poetic," he said.[13] Her outfits were coordinated down to the earrings, and, until her later years, when she could no longer manage it, she wore large, dramatic custom-made hats. A Cincinnati magazine once dubbed her "the Lady with the Hat."[14]

In 1937, when a disastrous flood hit Cincinnati, Helen was so concerned about the maids at her hotel that she gave out cookies, fruit, and juice every morning. But it was a difficult time for her too. Her office was closed initially, which meant no paycheck, and when the company did reopen, the toilets didn't work. She couldn't even wash her hair because the local water was pumped full of chemicals for purification. "I could FRY DOUGHNUTS in it it is so oily," she said.[15]

In 1956, Gibson moved its facilities from downtown to suburban Amberley Village, and Helen had to take a company bus to work. She boarded the bus every morning carrying a small white towel to sit on, which she placed on a seat behind the driver.[16] When she got to Gibson, she paused for a brief moment of personal meditation before entering. According to a story she liked to tell, a young boy saw her standing in front of the building pounding her fist into her hand one day. He asked what she was doing. "I was telling God 'if you don't get down here real soon, just for once, and straighten things out, you better not come at all.'"[17]

Helen's fame as a greeting card poet grew steadily, primarily because of her humorous verse, but her inspirational writing started attracting attention too. "The Christmas Guest," a poem based on one of her grandmother's stories, and another entitled

"Heart Gifts" became hits. A Gibson executive suggested she sign her most successful cards, a first for a woman.

Rice's fame soared when someone sent one of her cards, "The Priceless Gift of Christmas," to the performer known as Aladdin on *The Lawrence Welk Show*. He decided to do a dramatic rendering of it in December 1960, and it became a huge success. Welk asked for it to be turned into a song, and viewers wrote in for copies.[18]

Welk was so impressed with Rice that he and Aladdin arranged to have dinner with her in June 1961 while they were in town playing Cincinnati Gardens.[19] Over the next several years, four more of her poems were presented on *The Lawrence Welk Show*, and thousands of copies were requested by viewers. Gibson rushed to make Helen Steiner Rice greeting cards to meet the demand. By 1962, her inspirational verse had become big business for Gibson.

"The Praying Hands" and other Christmas verses were extremely popular, and other types of cards succeeded as well. "When I Must Leave You," a condolence poem written at the time of her mother's death, became a big seller as a sympathy card, and her tribute to John F. Kennedy, as well as one to John Glenn's mother after his historic space flight, were also well received. Paper booklets of her work were compiled and sold by the thousands. Helen even attracted international attention.

Helen Steiner Rice was a celebrity, and there were huge demands for public appearances as well as large amounts of fan mail to answer. She tried to respond to every letter herself and often offered personal advice or wrote verses to comfort people who were experiencing difficulties. She was sometimes referred to as the "Dear Abby" of the greeting card business.[20]

In 1967, Helen's first hardcover book, *Just for You*, was published by Doubleday,[21] and several dozen hardcover and paperback collections of inspirational verse, published by the F. H. Revell Co., followed. Thousands of copies sold. Helen continued working at Gibson, but the demands of managing all her appearances and other responsibilities were great. Finally, in 1971, she retired as Gibson greeting card editor, but, unable to bring herself to leave Gibson, she stayed on as a consultant and maintained an office there. A few years later, she faced another adjustment. In early 1974, at seventy-five, she was forced to leave her home when the Gibson Hotel was torn down. She moved into the nearby Cincinnati Club.[22]

Rice struggled with health issues as she aged, but managed to write an autobiography, *In the Vineyard of the Lord,* which was published in 1979. Also about that time, a friend, former Cincinnati mayor Gene Ruehlmann, helped her set up a charitable foundation. She had donated proceeds from her books to several churches for years, but she wanted to make sure the underprivileged benefited after she was gone. The Helen Steiner Rice Foundation is still in existence. It now operates under the auspices of the Greater Cincinnati Foundation, splitting its proceeds between Cincinnati and her hometown of Lorain.[23] The foundation has published a number of collections of her work to add to its holdings. Among them are several that combine Rice's poetry with the paintings and illustrations of Georgetown, Ohio, native John A. Ruthven, an acclaimed artist and founder of Wildlife International.[24]

In April of 1980, Rice took a bad fall, breaking a hip and a wrist as she got out of a car at Gibson Greeting Cards. She moved to the Franciscan Terrace retirement home in Wyoming, a Cincinnati suburb, and the next month the city of Cincinnati declared May 19 "Helen Steiner Rice Day" in honor of her eightieth birthday.[25] Both Pope John Paul II and President Jimmy Carter sent greetings. In March of the following year, Sister Jean Patrice Harrington, S.C., president of the College of Mount St. Joseph, came to Franciscan Terrace to bestow on the woman who had had to forgo college an honorary doctor of humane letters degree. Sister Jean acknowledged Rice's efforts to support women as well as her dedication "to high ideals and a humane concern for others." Rice died a month later.[26]

Helen Steiner Rice greeting cards still sell briskly, as do her gift items and her books, which have been reprinted many times. Her own life was difficult, but, as the president of Gibson pointed out at the time of her death, the dynamic little lady with the big hats and the contagious smile had a special quality in her writing that touched people and gave heart to her countless readers.[27] She continues to inspire.

CHAPTER NINETEEN

ANOTHER SPRING, ANOTHER POET

A photo says it all. A handful of good-looking young men and their attractive, well-dressed young wives pose in front of a Mount Airy picnic table piled to overflowing with martini shakers and half-empty bottles of gin and vermouth. Their eyes are lit with intelligence and excitement, and everyone is smiling. There's a campfire in the background, and darkness is falling.

The shoes, the clothes, and the Mamie Eisenhower–style hair-dos all suggest another time, and indeed it was. It was May 22, 1953, a postwar evening filled with food, drink, and literary repartee in the company of the English poet Stephen Spender. It was an era unknown to most Cincinnatians of later decades, a period that might be called Cincinnati's golden age of poetry.[1]

It began in 1951, when the University of Cincinnati launched the Elliston Poet-in-Residence Program. For more than a decade, the Elliston program flourished, each year bringing a notable English or American poet to spend the entire spring semester in Cincinnati. Embraced by some of the city's most prominent families, the poets gave campus readings and lectures and immersed themselves in a social life reminiscent of Tolstoy's Moscow.

Of course, the Elliston program isn't dead; the university still brings Elliston poets to campus. But sixty years ago it was something else. It was a time filled with intellectual debate, late-night skinny-dipping, and anecdotes delectable enough for literary biographers. Robert Lowell, John Berryman, John Betjeman, and many other literary lions left their mark on Cincinnati. And Cincinnati, it seems, left its mark on them as well.

The story begins, not with the Elliston lectures themselves, but with their benefactor, a woman named George Elliston. Born in 1883, Elliston grew up in Mount Sterling, Kentucky, and graduated from Covington High School, where she chose to stick with the masculine name her parents had given her. After graduation, she joined the staff of the *Cincinnati Times-Star* in a day when female reporters were confined to weddings and society events. It wasn't long, however, before she was climbing out of second-story windows with stolen photos and covering news in the city's red light district. Exceptionally tenacious and innovative, she was able to lock in stories no one else could, including an interview with Anna Marie Hahn, the first woman to die in Cincinnati's electric chair. She also regularly beat out her male competitors for plum assignments: the Paris Exposition and the eruption of a new volcano in Mexico among them. And then, in 1909, having made her mark as a reporter, she assumed the powerful post of society editor.[2]

But George Elliston was not just a successful newspaperwoman; she was also a poet. Her poems were syndicated in newspapers and magazines, reproduced in British and American anthologies, translated into foreign languages, and set to music by various composers. Four hardbound volumes of her verse still grace the shelves of the Public Library of Cincinnati and Hamilton County.

A slender woman with luminous dark eyes and wisps of nondescript hair that slipped from her signature cloche, Elliston lived like a pauper. She had an eighteen-dollar-a-month cold-water flat on a shabby block of West Fourth Street, and the staff at one restaurant called her the "gelatin lady" because she never ordered anything else. Her friends took pity on her Salvation Army dress and gave her clothes.

Though reluctant to spend money on ordinary things, the lively Miss Elliston loved parties and frequently entertained in Cincinnati and in Morrow as well, where she bought a hundred-year-old log cabin with a large barn for her amateur theatricals. There was even a hint of scandal about the activities there, which included such goings on as visits by unsupervised male callers. Elliston did marry in 1907, but her husband lived in St. Louis, and, though she moved there at first, she soon returned to Cincinnati, quietly resuming her newspaper job. She and her husband remained on cordial terms and never divorced.

What most people didn't know about "poor George" was that she was saving her meager hundred-dollar-a-week salary and discreetly investing in property under her married name. When she died in Madisonville in 1946, Cincinnati was stunned to learn that she had left the astonishing sum of $250,000 to the University of Cincinnati, designated for the establishment of a chair "to encourage and promote the study and composition of poetry."[3]

At the time Elliston's will was read, the poet Robert Frost happened to be lecturing at the university. "Where is there such another chair in the United States?" he asked the newspaper. And he was right: Elliston's gift was a rarity, which enabled the school to create a program that became the envy of the literary world.[4]

The task of managing the Elliston bequest fell to the head of the English Department, the correct and proper William S. Clark II, Frost's friend and former student. A scholarly man sometimes described as a "gentle dictator," Clark took his job seriously. "His mission, as he conceived it—he was a very New Englandish sort of person—was to bring culture to the Midwest," recalled Dr. Keith Stewart, a retired English professor, in 2003. "He and his wife Gladys held the responsibility very close to their chests. No one knew the name of the Elliston poet until he announced it." The Clarks not only handpicked the poets but also traveled to Europe to vet them if necessary. Then they'd negotiate the contracts, choose the lodging, and arrange the schedules.[5]

As Clark envisioned the program, the poet would spend a full semester in Cincinnati, usually arriving in January or February. For three thousand dollars a month, a handsome sum in 1951, the poet would present six or eight programs and conduct a workshop or two. The lectures and the workshops were open to the public, giving the university an opportunity to win influential friends.[6]

The poet would also, Clark decided, be wined and dined.

And thus enters thirty-three-year-old Elizabeth Bettman, one of Clark's friends and then the wife of future judge Gilbert Bettman. A dark-haired beauty from an eastern blue-blood family, Liz Bettman spoke French and was an accomplished hostess. Quick, vivacious, and, by all accounts, brilliant, she knew her literature; she later became a professor at the University of Cincinnati's University College. She was also radical in her political and social views for a resident of a conservative Midwestern town—she was actually arrested at one point for taking black children into what was then segregated Coney Island.[7]

Although they were an unlikely pair, Dr. Clark and Mrs. Bettman developed an elaborate plan to roll out the red carpet for visiting poets by enlisting the hospitality of a variety of people both on and off campus. The university defrayed some of the cost, but twenty or so wealthy and prominent arts supporters, people with celebrated Cincinnati names such as Wulsin, Fleischmann, Strauss, Emery, and Lanier, were also tapped for assistance. On the university side, there were another dozen couples, including five who formed an inner circle. In addition to the Clarks and the Bettmans, the close-knit cadre included philosophy professor Van Meter Ames and his wife, Betty; English professor George H. Ford and his wife, Pat; and classics professor J. Alister Cameron and his wife, a couple known affectionately as Hamish and Puggy.

Despite the best-laid plans, the launch of the program was not auspicious. The first poet, set to arrive in February 1951, was to be none other than the acclaimed T. S. Eliot, but at the last minute Eliot canceled, and Clark had to scramble for a replacement. On such short notice he was forced to settle for a poet of lesser distinction: Robert P. Tristram Coffin.[8]

The first lecture was held in Wilson Memorial Hall, and about four hundred people, many times the typical crowd for similar events today, braved a snowstorm to attend.[9] Apparently Coffin, a kindly man from Maine, was well liked and enjoyed himself so much he volunteered to paint a scene of a southern landscape in the university's Stephen Foster Room (it has since been covered up). But his readings ran on and on. At one lecture, Mrs. Claude Lotspeich, a founder of the Seven Hills School, reportedly interrupted, "And that would be a good one to end on, Mr. Coffin." Mr. Coffin realized he'd met his match and sat down.[10]

The following year was a different scene altogether. Clark issued an invitation to John Berryman, who later won a Pulitzer Prize for *The Dream Songs,* and things got rolling in earnest.

Berryman was a pixie-like figure with a slight body, long hands, and a quizzical face. Warm and outgoing, he was so loud and manic that Ford described the season as "Berrymania."[11] Instead of the expected six appearances, Berryman insisted on giving seventeen, energetically reading and lecturing with his coat off and sleeves rolled up, flashing a pair of fashionable braces.[12] He was a heavy drinker, and his drinking set a tone for the poetry season for years to come. From then on, there were martinis. Lots of martinis.[13]

It was also during Berryman's visit that members of the group took up partying until five or six in the morning. Berryman's wife loved to dance, so carpets were rolled up in private homes. Some members even went skinny-dipping, ditching their bathing suits for a dip in the Walnut Hills swimming pool of Iphigene Bettman, Gilbert Bettman's mother and a prominent local newspaper columnist.[14]

Unfortunately, no details of the pool parties emerged from a host of interviews in 2003, although Pat Ford, the only surviving member of the inner circle, described them as innocent enough. However, Ames, a published poet himself, did recount many of the group's activities in a meticulously kept, unpublished journal. An entry from 1952 gives a flavor:

FIGURE 19.1 John Berryman (*second from left*) with Cincinnati professors J. Alister Cameron, Van Meter Ames, Michael Krouse, and George H. Ford. *Courtesy of Pat Ford*

Cincinnati, Sunday 30 March 1952. How full of living, seeing our friends over and over, the days have been! A week ago last Saturday, with the Berrymans at the Fords'. Sunday my philosophy of religion students over in the afternoon. Then dinner with Billy & Elsa Strauss, the Berrymans, Levines, et al, being there, and the Camerons . . . Berryman came over Tuesday evening after his wife had gone to bed. We laughed and laughed and he got drunk. It was in my study, where I had gone to bed to read. . . . Yesterday Hamish and Puggy drove the Berrymans and us to see the Carl Strauss house. . . . Then to the Ransohoff house to see Toscanini, the 9th Symphony, his last television appearance, but it had been cancelled. . . . then dinner at the Camerons' on the pheasants Gil Bettman had shot, and he and Liz were there with Danny and the Berrymans, and there was broccoli with a fine sauce, and Eileen seemed embarrassed at John's loudness.

The days that followed were a smorgasbord of debates on Plato and Sophocles, intimate Sunday dinner parties with mint juleps in Clifton homes, elegant soirees in Indian Hill, and occasional lighthearted readings of verse written by Berryman in honor of his Cincinnati friends. There was also the occasional altercation. For example, Berryman and Ames's wife had some sort of an argument at a dinner party when Berryman was "taking himself so seriously." However, Betty Ames finally got the upper hand. "With him," she told her husband, "you have to terrify or be terrified!"[15]

Despite all the partying, Berryman, like many of the visiting poets, produced a substantial amount of serious work while staying in the city, including a significant portion of "Homage to Mistress Bradstreet," a poem nominated for the Pulitzer Prize in 1956. According to John Haffenden's *Life of John Berryman,* the interlude was an important factor in his development as a poet. "The peculiar success of Cincinnati was that it energized and absorbed Berryman. . . . Also, lionized as never before in his career, he was at last able to take the coveted role of a celebrity, and to indulge to the utmost both the courtly and the raffish sides of his personality."[16]

With Berryman's visit the die was cast for more than a decade. A parade of famous poets, including not only Spender, Lowell, and Betjeman but also Peter Viereck, Robert Frost, Randall Jarrell, and Karl Shapiro, came to the city each year. They lived in Vernon Manor, a stately 1920s apartment hotel that was near campus, and generally lectured in Room 127 (a large classroom) of McMicken Hall. It was not unusual for crowds of several hundred people, "town" outnumbering "gown," to flock to the lectures to hear often esoteric topics.[17] One of Spender's programs, for example, was entitled "Despair in Eliot's *Wasteland* and Orwell's *1984.*"[18]

The poets would also drop into brown-bag lunches in the English Department and mingle with the faculty. Over time, it became customary for the Elliston poets to attend meetings of the Jolly

Boys, a group of university professors who got together in members' homes to have beer and sandwiches and read articles they'd written.[19] Oddly, the poets were also expected to speak at Thursday gatherings set up by the late Maurice Levine of the Psychiatry Department to develop well-rounded psychiatrists. These were called "perhaps seminars"—perhaps this or perhaps that.[20]

Then the poets would find themselves caught up in a round of social events that were often custom tailored to fit their interests. For example, John Betjeman, the seventh Elliston lecturer and later England's poet laureate, was a noted authority on architecture, so he was taken on tours of the city by Danny Ransohoff, one of Cincinnati's best-known civic boosters and historians. At the conclusion of his visit, Betjeman wrote a lengthy newspaper article praising the city and proclaiming the virtues of City Hall, Mount Adams, Columbia Parkway, the Frank Lloyd Wright house in Clifton, and other sights. However, he was appalled by the city's slums, ending his article, "Oh loved Cincinnati / I bid thee farewell, / Thy heights are perfection / Thy basin is hell."[21]

Another revealing story about Betjeman comes from Walter E. Langsam, son of a University of Cincinnati president, who recalls prevailing upon his parents to throw a dinner party for the Betjemans. The president's home at the time was a grand Italian stucco house with a tile roof in Clifton. Langsam's mother was an excellent hostess, with a passion for beautiful flowers and a policy of never using any recipe twice. About a dozen people were invited for the lavish evening, and Betjeman was accompanied by his wife, Lady Penelope. "She was dumpy and dowdy," Langsam reported later. "He was dumpy too, but cute.

"The first person Lady Penelope saw when she arrived was Marion Becker [author of *The Joy of Cooking*]. They were both wearing shoes that were early Birkenstocks. They immediately recognized each other as soul mates, threw their arms around each other, and spent the whole evening together."

After dinner, the Langsams gave their twenty-two-year-old son a chance to visit with the poet. "I had a Whistler etching. . . . I was curious about that. I think I took him upstairs to see it. He said it was a view from Fleet Street. . . . But he sort of dismissed me. He wanted to talk about death." Betjeman had a theory that Americans were terrified of death and couldn't bear to speak of it. When Langsam said he'd never been to a funeral, Betjeman couldn't believe it. "He said I *must* have. The more I denied it, the more he insisted."[22]

Stephen Spender, the 1953 invitee, was one of the most popular Elliston lecturers—once he finally made it to town. After his appointment was announced, word spread around Cincinnati that he had been a Communist, and there was a local outcry, jeopardizing his visa. University of Cincinnati president Raymond Walters, with the help of a university board member, asked Senator Robert Taft to intervene with the U.S. State Department. Spender got his visa.[23]

Sir Stephen, a gentle six-foot, three-inch Englishman who was knighted in 1983, recounts in his published journals the story of a Cincinnati evening when he was invited to a dinner party following a concert. About 2 a.m. "a lady psychologist" started describing a treatment that would help mental patients by reverting them to the state of babies. Before they knew it, the whole group was lying on the floor listening to soothing music while a gentle voice crooned, "Baby is in the cot. Mother loves baby. Mother pats baby." And, added Spender, "We were not drunk or anything. The incident was carried out in a perfectly sober, business-like way."[24]

There were, however, occasions during Spender's visit when a considerable amount of alcohol *was* consumed. Shortly before he was to leave the city, he planned a picnic for the Cincinnatians who had entertained him during his stay. Liz Bettman helped him order food and drink and to reserve Ponderosa Ridge in Mount Airy Forest. When the appointed day arrived, the weather forecast was so dire that Spender spent the afternoon writing European friends that he was likely to be whisked away by tornadoes. The storms never materialized, however, and the close-knit group sat around a campfire drinking martinis, chatting about scholarly work, and bantering with Spender. They also posed for the now long-lost picnic photo that Bettman family members recalled as perfectly capturing the tenor of the times.[25]

The occasion was typical for the Elliston series, with strong friendships inevitably being forged between the community and "the poets," as they came to be called. For example, Robert Lowell told Ames and his wife how lucky they were to have such friends, "a society that cannot be equaled for charm anywhere in the United States." Betjeman once contemplated the forty or so people around him and noted that he did not think such a large group could be gathered in Birmingham, England. "Perhaps 20 in Belfast, 30 in Dublin."[26]

All the Elliston visits of the period were memorable in one way or another, but if there is one that stands out, it is Robert Lowell's residency in 1954. Lowell's tenure as an Elliston poet presents a dramatic example not only of the relationships forged but also of how the visits worked themselves into literary history. Winner of two Pulitzer Prizes and fourth lecturer in the Elliston series, Lowell was a handsome Boston aristocrat who suffered from mental illness much of his life. A massive man, six-foot four and 220 or 230 pounds, he was so revered that one of his former Harvard students described him in an interview as "like the Dali Lama [*sic*]—the second coming of Christ."[27] Barely a week after Lowell assumed the Elliston post, his mother fell ill. He quickly left for Italy to see her, but she died before he arrived. After he buried her, he returned to Cincinnati and promptly announced he was divorcing his wife to marry an Italian. His wife, Elizabeth Hardwick, fled the city.[28]

At that point, Lowell became increasingly unstable. He talked nonstop, insulted a guest at a party held in his honor, and jumped from a moving cab to keep from paying the fare. He was also extremely intense when he lectured, laughing too heartily at his own jokes and going so far as to read the footnotes. He started frequenting the Gayety, a local strip club, and sometimes visited stripper Rose La Rose several times a day.[29] Pat Ford remembered having Lowell to dinner during the period, but, she added, "I found him sufficiently disturbing that I was not leaving my children with him . . . not that he would have hurt them."[30]

Gilbert Bettman Jr., the Bettmans' son and now a California resident, recalled an evening when his father, Lowell, and several other people piled into the Bettmans' Willys jeep to collect a number of bookcases at a local office. "Lowell was completely useless. While they worked all night, Lowell went around and had lengthy conversations with all the women cleaning the offices."[31]

As Lowell's illness became more and more apparent, Chairman Clark took matters in hand. Summoning the biggest and strongest of the English faculty to his office, he directed them to sit on the front row at Lowell's lectures to forestall any violence.[32] And Lowell did have a breakdown at one of the lectures. He lapsed into a rambling ovation on Hitler that seemed to extol the superman ideology. No violence erupted, but the event was so disturbing that his sixth and final lecture was canceled.[33]

As Lowell became increasingly unstable, his wife attempted to get him into medical treatment, but the Clarks and the Bettmans tried to protect him, and the Bettmans even wrote letters of encouragement to the Italian woman. Lowell dubbed Bettman his "lawyer," and Hardwick returned to the city to get a court order to have her husband committed.[34]

Valerie Foulkes, part of the poetry crowd and then a member of the university's English Department, reported that Lowell promised to take her to a burlesque show because she'd never seen one, but at the last minute she got a call saying he couldn't come. He was being carted off to the hospital.

Lowell was admitted to Jewish Hospital, where he was given warm bath treatments and electroshock therapy. By then, the Bettmans had realized how ill he was and acknowledged they'd made a mistake.

But their role in the whole affair did not escape notice by Lowell's biographers. In *Robert Lowell: A Biography*, the distinguished Cincinnati couple is described by one of Ian Hamilton's sources as "weak-minded" because they failed to exercise better judgment.[35]

Sometime in the mid- to late 1960s, the Elliston Lectures started to change. Poets still came to Cincinnati every spring ("another spring, another poet," as Ames once noted in his journal), but the poetry season began to lose its allure. Clark retired in 1966, and his successors made changes that altered the complexion of the program. Part of the Elliston money was redirected to fellowships, leaving fewer dollars to attract the top-tier poets. And more emphasis was placed on student involvement, less on socializing in the community.[36]

It also became increasingly difficult to attract poets for such a long residency. Most of them eventually took teaching posts, as they generally do today, and couldn't leave their jobs for a full semester.

James V. Cummins, curator of the Elliston poetry collection since 1975, concluded in an interview that the university simply ran out of the ultrafamous. "In the '60s, the people were perfectly respectable but not Robert Lowell." During his own tenure, he adds, "We've had a *Who's Who* of poetry, but no one was interested." The world also changed. The wild and free postwar period in which the lectures started, when life was gay and people felt like celebrating, gave way to more serious times. More women joined the workforce and became too busy to entertain. Poetry lost some of its popular appeal.

And, of course, Cincinnati's hip literati, that unique group of well-read, fun-loving bohemians who fueled a special time in the city's history, grew old. Gradually they partied less, stopped going to lectures, and finally faded away. The legacy of George Elliston, the eccentric, fun-loving newspaperwoman who adored poetry, lives on. But in a different way.

AFTERWORD

A nd the story goes on. About the same time Helen Steiner
Rice died, so did two other writers with significant Cincinnati connections. One was Rod Serling (1924–1975), creator of
the famous *Twilight Zone* series. Serling lived in the Wyoming area
of the city in the early 1950s and started his professional broadcast
career at WLW radio and WKRC-TV. He also sold scripts to Cincinnati's illustrious Crosley Broadcasting Corporation.

Then there's Marion Rombauer Becker (1903–1976) of the *Joy
of Cooking* dynasty, who makes a brief appearance in the Elliston
chapter. She revised and updated several editions of her mother's
Joy of Cooking, one of the best-selling cookbooks of all time, in a
house off Newtown Road above Clough Pike in Anderson Town-
ship. After that, she went on to write her own version of *Joy,* and
then her son Ethan carried on the family business in the same house
until he moved to Tennessee in 2004.

Since that time there have been a number of other prominent
writers with Cincinnati connections: native Cincinnatian Kenneth
Koch (1925–2002), the poet, playwright, and professor who became
a prominent member of the New York School of poetry; Ross Feld
(1947–2001), novelist and fiction reviewer for *Kirkus Reviews,* who
spent his last twenty years in Cincinnati; and Kay Boyle (1902–1992),
writer, educator, political activist, and European correspondent for
the *New Yorker,* who grew up and studied in Cincinnati.

And, of course, the Cincinnati tradition continues today. I chose not to include living writers in this book, both because their best work may still lie before them and because of the difficulty of assessing their accomplishments without benefit of distance in time. But there are quite a few, and they nicely bring the city's literary interest up to the present. Among them are native Cincinnatian Michael Cunningham, winner of the Pulitzer Prize for *The Hours;* novelist Thomas Berger, author of *Little Big Man,* who was born in the city and studied at the University of Cincinnati; Nikki Giovanni, the widely acclaimed poet, who grew up in Lincoln Heights; Stephen Birmingham, author of more than thirty books, who is now retired on Mount Adams; and Edmund White, writer and cultural critic, who spent significant periods of his childhood in the city.

Others are Western Hills native Gail Collins, columnist, author, and the first woman to serve as editorial page editor of the *New York Times;* poets Donald Bogen and Norman Finkelstein, who teach at local universities; up-and-coming novelists Curtis Sittenfeld and Brock Clarke; author and educator Sharon M. Draper; and children's book author/illustrator Will Hillenbrand. And then there's the multitalented Wendell Berry from nearby Port Royal, Kentucky; nonfiction writer Ann Hagedorn, who lives in Ripley, Ohio; and . . . well, the list is lengthy.

On a different note, the city still enjoys the Ropes program, an endowment established more than a hundred years ago to support comparative literature. Focused on benefiting both University of Cincinnati students and the community at large, the program regularly brings to town such eminent writers as Richard Powers, E. L. Doctorow, Christopher Hitchens, and Pulitzer Prize–winning poet Richard Howard. Howard, by the way, has spent a substantial amount of time in Cincinnati because he has also served as an Elliston poet.

Cincinnati has famously proved itself in the area of literary inspiration or subject matter too. For example, Nobel Prize winner

Toni Morrison's *Beloved* (1987) is focused on the Margaret Garner case, the real-life story of a woman who killed her child in Cincinnati to prevent her return to slavery. Morrison also wrote the libretto for a 2005 opera called *Margaret Garner*.

I know this list is incomplete and that there are many stories, both past and present, that remain untold. And I'm sure there are Cincinnatians writing today who are unknown to me but who are quietly moving toward places of distinction. I apologize in advance for the omissions, but I offer one consolation: plenty of material remains for another volume. Who knows? We may see Authors Grove rebuilt yet.

NOTES

PREFACE

1. Ohio's Arbor Day is believed to be the first planting of memorial trees in the country.

CHAPTER I: A TROLLOPE! A TROLLOPE!

1. Donald Smalley, introduction to Frances Milton Trollope, *Domestic Manners of the Americans,* ed. Donald Smalley (New York: Knopf, 1949), xvii–xix. The description of Mrs. Trollope is from Cincinnatian Timothy Flint, cited in Una Pope-Hennessy, *Three English Women in America* (London: E. Benn, 1929), 28.

2. Pope-Hennessy, *Three English Women,* 42–43.

3. Smalley, introduction to Trollope, *Domestic Manners,* xvii–xviii, xxxvi.

4. Trollope says in *Domestic Manners* that this occurred at the Washington Hotel. The 1825 *Hall City Directory* mentions a Washington Hotel on Seventh Street between Main and Walnut. However, the innkeeper in question is believed to be Joseph H. Cromwell, who had a reputation for tyrannical behavior. He was the innkeeper of the Cincinnati Hotel at 6 West Front Street (the corner of Front and Broadway). See *Cincinnati Enquirer,* November 9, 1997, E10.

5. Pamela Neville-Sington, *Fanny Trollope: The Life and Adventures of a Clever Woman* (New York: Viking, 1998), 124.

6. Pope-Hennessey, *Three English Women,* 55.

7. Smalley, introduction to Trollope, *Domestic Manners,* xx–xxi; Neville-Sington, *Fanny Trollope,* 125.

8. Pope-Hennessey, *Three English Women,* 63; John Clubbe, *Cincinnati Observed: Architecture and History* (Columbus: Ohio State University Press, 1992), 237. According to *In Memory of Elizabeth Haven Appleton* (Cincinnati: Robert Clark, 1891), 118–19, the house was situated in the yard of the Hamilton Road Pottery, which is listed in the 1870 *Williams' Cincinnati Directory* as owned by Frederick Dallas.

9. Thomas Adolphus Trollope, *What I Remember,* 2 vols. (New York: Harper and Brothers, 1888–90), 116.

10. F. Trollope, *Domestic Manners,* 105, 99–100.

11. Smalley, introduction to Trollope, *Domestic Manners,* xxxviii.

12. Neville-Sington, *Fanny Trollope,* 130, 146.

13. J. Roger Newstedt, "Frances Trollope in Cincinnati: The 'Infernal Regions' and the Bizarre Bazaar, 1828–1830," *Queen City Heritage* 57, no. 4 (1999): 39.

14. Smalley, introduction to Trollope, *Domestic Manners,* xxxi.

15. T. Trollope, *What I Remember,* 123.

16. The Western Museum, founded in 1818, failed in 1854 but was revived in the 1870s as the Cincinnati Society of Natural History and continues as the Museum of Natural History and Science at the Cincinnati Museum Center. Owen Findsen, "Hell of an Idea Saved Once-Boring 1880s Museum," *Cincinnati Enquirer,* September 24, 1995, G9.

17. F. Trollope, *Domestic Manners,* 74.

18. *The Cincinnati Directory for the Year 1829* (Cincinnati: Robinson and Fairbank, 1829), 176–77.

19. Smalley, introduction to Trollope, *Domestic Manners,* xl.

20. *Cincinnati City Directory for the Year 1829,* 177.

21. Smalley, introduction to Trollope, *Domestic Manners,* xlv.

22. Neville-Sington, *Fanny Trollope,* 141–42; Smalley, introduction to Trollope, *Domestic Manners,* xliii. Spermaceti is a waxy substance obtained from marine mammals, especially sperm whales.

23. Smalley, introduction to Trollope, *Domestic Manners,* xlv–li. Hervieu included in the painting many local citizens who had not been on hand when Lafayette visited the city in 1825. The present whereabouts of the painting is unknown.

24. Smalley, introduction to Trollope, *Domestic Manners,* app. B, 437.

25. *Domestic Manners* was launched March 19, 1832. Smalley, introduction to Trollope, *Domestic Manners,* viii.

26. Pope-Hennessey, *Three English Women,* 16.

27. David Stradling, *Cincinnati: From River City to Highway Metropolis* (Charleston, SC: Arcadia, 2003), 26.

28. Fanny Trollope had seven children, but one died at birth and another in childhood. Brenda Ayers, "Apis Trollopiana: An Introduction to the Nearly Extinct Trollope," in *Frances Trollope and the Novel of Social Change,* ed. Brenda Ayers (Westport, CT: Greenwood Press, 2001), 4.

29. Smalley, introduction to Trollope, *Domestic Manners,* lxx.

30. Teresa Ransom, *Fanny Trollope: A Remarkable Life* (New York: St. Martin's Press, 1995), 87; "From the Ohio Mechanics Institute to the OMI College of Applied Science of the University of Cincinnati," http://www .omicas175.uc.edu/pdf/timeline.pdf; Clubbe, *Cincinnati Observed,* 131. Anthony Trollope came to America in 1862 to retrace his mother's footsteps and correct what he considered her "somewhat unjust" approach. He visited

Cincinnati, stayed at the Burnet House, saw what was by then a "sorry"-looking Bazaar, and had his own encounter with Cincinnati pigs. See an unpublished Cincinnati Literary Club paper from 1929 entitled "Anthony Trollope in Cincinnati" by Simeon Moses Johnson, or Trollope's book, *North America*.

CHAPTER 2: BUCKEYES, SEMI-COLONS, AND OTHER LITERATI

1. The first newspaper was the *Centinel of the North-Western Territory*. *Cincinnati: A Guide to the Queen City and Its Neighbors* (Cincinnati: Wiesen-Hart Press, 1943), 149.

2. John P. Foote, *Memoirs of the Life of Samuel E. Foote* (Cincinnati: Robert Clarke, 1860), 178. Several literary organizations predate the Semi-Colon Club, including the Literary Society (1818), the Franklin Society (1825), and the Cincinnati Lyceum (1830). There was also something called the Inquisition, which focused on discussion and papers about public issues. See Charles Theodore Greve, *Centennial History of Cincinnati and Representative Citizens*, 2 vols. (Chicago: Biographical, 1904), vol. 1.

3. Louis L. Tucker, "The Semi-Colon Club of Cincinnati," *Ohio History* 73 (1965): 13–15.

4. Greve, *Centennial History of Cincinnati*, 1:648.

5. Tucker, "Semi-Colon Club," 17.

6. Ibid., 18.

7. Names of the members have been drawn from several sources, including Tucker, "Semi-Colon Club," 16, and W. H. Venable, *Beginnings of Literary Culture in the Ohio Valley: Historical and Biographical Sketches* (Cincinnati: R. Clarke, 1891), 418.

8. J. Roger Newstedt, "The Literary Flowering of Early Cincinnati, 1788–1849," in *The Literary Club of Cincinnati, 1849–1999* (Cincinnati: Literary Club of Cincinnati, 2001), 56–60; Greve, *Centennial History of Cincinnati*, 1:650.

9. Edward D. Mansfield says that "Dr. Drake was himself head of the circle." Mansfield, *Memoirs of the Life and Services of Daniel Drake, M.D.* (Cincinnati: Applegate, 1855), 225; J. Christian Bay, *Dr. Daniel Drake, 1785–1852* (Louisville: Filson Club, 1933), 3.

10. Cincinnati was founded in December 1788 by Israel Ludlow and about twenty others. Initially, the city was named Losantiville, but shortly afterwards it was renamed Cincinnati by the new governor of the Northwest Territory.

11. For detailed information on Drake's life, see Mansfield, *Memoirs*, and Richard Farrell, "Daniel Drake: The Ohio Valley's Benjamin Franklin," *Cincinnati Historical Society Bulletin* 23 (October 1965): 243–56.

12. Daniel Drake, *Natural and Statistical View, or Picture of Cincinnati and the Miami Country* (Cincinnati: Looker and Wallace, 1815).

13. According to Greve, *Centennial History of Cincinnati*, 1:645, Drake's home was on Vine Street at the corner of Baker.

14. Tucker, "Semi-Colon Club," 15.

15. Emmet Field Horine, *Daniel Drake (1785–1852): Pioneer Physician of the Midwest* (Philadelphia: University of Pennsylvania Press, 1961), 380.

16. Bay, *Dr. Daniel Drake*, 13.

17. Greve, *Centennial History of Cincinnati*, 1:646.

18. Horine, *Daniel Drake*, 238–39.

19. Harriet Martineau, *Retrospect of Western Travel*, 2 vols. (London: Saunders and Otley, 1838), 2:50.

20. Tucker, "Semi-Colon Club," 15; Edward D. Mansfield, *Personal Memories: Social, Political, and Literary* (Cincinnati: Robert Clarke, 1879), 262.

21. Mansfield, *Memoirs*, 224–25.

22. Horine, *Daniel Drake*, 379.

23. Nina Mjagkij, ed., *Organizing Black America: An Encyclopedia of African American Associations* (New York: Garland, 2001), 147.

CHAPTER 3: THE LITTLE WOMAN WHO WROTE THE BOOK

1. Barbara Anne White, *The Beecher Sisters* (New Haven: Yale University Press, 2003), 11–12. The quote from Lincoln has been widely reported in a variety of sources.

2. Joan D. Hedrick, *Harriet Beecher Stowe: A Life* (New York: Oxford University Press, 1994), 72–73, 83; Debby Applegate, *The Most Famous Man in America: The Biography of Henry Ward Beecher* (New York: Doubleday, 2006), 110.

3. B. White, *Beecher Sisters*, 12–13.

4. James Albert Green, "The Beecher Family in Cincinnati," September 19, 1949. The Literary Club of Cincinnati Papers, vol. 72, 1. Cincinnati Historical Society.

5. Annie Fields, ed., *Life and Letters of Harriet Beecher Stowe* (Boston: Houghton, Mifflin, 1897), 80.

6. Nathaniel Wright, *Memorial Address Delivered Before the Second Presbyterian Church and Society of Cincinnati* (Cincinnati: Robert Clarke 1872), 22. For the location of the church, see the 1834 *Deming Cincinnati City Directory*. The McAlpin buildings now house condominiums.

7. Applegate, *Most Famous Man in America*, 117; Catharine Beecher, *The Biographical Remains of Rev. George Beecher* (New York: Leavitt, Trow, 1844), 11–12.

8. The location of the school is listed in Greve, *Centennial History of Cincinnati*, 1:615 as Fourth and Sycamore, the former site of the Ryland School. It is also listed at that location in the 1834 *Deming Cincinnati City Directory*.

Other sources list it at Third and Plum Streets, but the Sycamore information is compelling. In addition to running the school, Catharine wrote several books in Cincinnati, including a cookbook entitled *Miss Beecher's Domestic Receipt Book*. It was published in 1847.

9. B. White, *Beecher Sisters*, 19. Harriet and Catharine lived downtown while running the school and boarded at a Mrs. S. Wright's (1834 *Deming Cincinnati City Directory*, 18). Mrs. Wright's address is not listed, but it is clear from the directory that she was a member of the Second Presbyterian Church, where Dr. Lyman Beecher was pastor.

10. "Harriet Beecher Stowe's Life," http://www.harrietbeecherstowecenter .org/; Hedrick, *Harriet Beecher Stowe*, 70.

11. Louis L. Tucker, "The Semi-Colon Club of Cincinnati," *Ohio History* 73 (1965): 24.

12. Harriet Beecher Stowe, *The Mayflower and Miscellaneous Writings* (Boston: Phillips, Sampson, 1855), 3–4.The acknowledgment did not appear in the original edition published in 1843 under the title *The Mayflower; or, Sketches of Scenes and Characters among the Descendants of the Pilgrims*. It was added to the 1855 edition.

13. Tucker, "Semi-Colon Club," 25.

14. Hedrick, *Harriet Beecher Stowe*, 98–99.The honeymoon is mentioned in a letter published in chapter 4 of *Life of Harriet Beecher Stowe*, compiled by Charles Edward Stowe (Boston: Houghton, Mifflin, 1891).

15. Hedrick, *Harriet Beecher Stowe*, 113, 125; Geoffrey J. Giglierano and Deborah A. Overmyer, *The Bicentennial Guide to Greater Cincinnati: A Portrait of Two Hundred Years* (Cincinnati: Cincinnati Historical Society, 1988), 178.

16. "Harriet Beecher Stowe: Incidents of Her Life in Cincinnati," *Cincinnati Commercial Tribune*, July 5, 1896, 18.

17. Hedrick, *Harriet Beecher Stowe*, 196–97.

18. For an extensive list of Stowe's articles and pamphlets, see Hedrick, *Harriet Beecher Stowe*, 476–77. Hedrick does not list the *Cincinnati Chronicle*, but Edward D. Mansfield believed that he published Stowe's first piece, a story he heard her read in Connecticut, while he was editor of the paper. He said the story was so good that listeners thought her father had written it. *Hamilton County, Ohio: As extracted from Henry Howe's Historical Collections of Ohio*, ed. Barbara Keyser Gargiulo (Milford, OH: Little Miami, 2005), 91.

19. "Stowe's Family," http://www.harrietbeecherstowecenter.org/; B. White, *Beecher Sisters*, 35.

20. Applegate, *Most Famous Man in America*, 111.

21. B. White, *Beecher Sisters*, 16–17.

22. Ann Hagedorn, *Beyond the River: The Untold Story of the Heroes of the Underground Railroad* (New York: Simon and Schuster, 2002), 68–73.

23. Hedrick, *Harriet Beecher Stowe,* 105–9.

24. Hagedorn, *Beyond the River,* 139.

25. Ibid., 120.

26. Hedrick, *Harriet Beecher Stowe,* 121.

27. Hagedorn, *Beyond the River,* 169.

28. Harriet Beecher Stowe, *The Key to Uncle Tom's Cabin* (Salem, NH: Ayer, 1987), 2–101. The famous Margaret Garner case, in which a woman murdered her two-year-old daughter to prevent the child from being returned to slavery, occurred in Cincinnati in 1856 and formed the basis of Toni Morrison's Pulitzer Prize–winning novel *Beloved.*

29. Hedrick, *Harriet Beecher Stowe,* 190–193, 208, 223.

30. Dale Patrick Brown, *Brilliance and Balderdash: Early Lectures at Cincinnati's Mercantile Library* (Cincinnati: Mercantile Library, 2007), 42.

31. "Charley's Death, One of the Happenings in a Walnut Hills House Made a Shrine," *Cincinnati Post,* December 22, 1943, 17.

32. There is no record of the whereabouts of Charley's grave. He was probably buried in a cemetery connected with Lane Theological Seminary in Walnut Hills, but Spring Grove Cemetery, where at least some of the graves from Walnut Hills were later moved, has no record of the baby. Spring Grove records do show that the graves of Eliza Stowe, Calvin's first wife, and Harriet Porter Beecher, Lyman's second wife, were moved there. It is logical to assume that the baby was originally buried near them, but whether his body was moved to Spring Grove when theirs were, or his grave has since been buried under Walnut Hills development, is impossible to say.

CHAPTER 4: LEASES, LECTURES, AND A LIBRARY

1. Unless specifically noted, the information in this chapter is drawn from Dale Patrick Brown, *Brilliance and Balderdash: Early Lectures at Cincinnati's Mercantile Library* (Cincinnati: Mercantile Library, 2007). The claim related to the Mercantile's status as the oldest continuously operating library west of Philadelphia is discussed in Robert C. Vitz, *At the Center: 175 Years at Cincinnati's Mercantile Library* (Cincinnati: Mercantile Library, 2010), 3n3.

2. The number of books in the collection was accurately ascertained in 2009 when the Mercantile digitized its catalogue. The collection had previously been thought to be much larger.

3. *History of the Young Men's Mercantile Library Association of Cincinnati, 1835–1935* (Cincinnati: Ebbert and Richardson, 1935), 5.

4. "Minutes," the Young Men's Mercantile Library Association, December 21, 1835; *History of the Young Men's Mercantile Library Association,* 16;

"Joseph S. Benham," *Ohio History* 29 (1920): 558–59; "Mercantile Law Class," *Cincinnati Daily Gazette,* January 4, 1836.

5. "Quadri-centennial" means the four hundredth rather than the twenty-fifth anniversary, but this was the term used. Pike's Opera House was on the south side of Fourth Street between Walnut and Vine, where the PNC Tower is now located. "Y.M.M.L. Association: Quadri-Centennial Anniversary," *Cincinnati Daily Gazette,* April 19, 1860.

6. "Minutes," the Young Men's Mercantile Library Association, January 31, 1860; *Annual Report,* the Young Men's Mercantile Library Association (Cincinnati: Young Men's Mercantile Library Association, 1860); "Y.M.M.L. Association. Quadri-Centennial Anniversary," *Cincinnati Daily Gazette,* April 19, 1860.

7. "Y.M.L.A." *Cincinnati Commercial Gazette,* April 19, 1885.

8. "Minutes," the Young Men's Mercantile Library Association, May 15, April 20, and May 17, 1910.

9. The Cincinnati Law College is now the University of Cincinnati College of Law. "Home-Like," *Cincinnati Times-Star,* May 3, 1910.

10. "Hostesses at Library Tea," *Cincinnati Times-Star,* November 14, 1934; "Dorothy Thompson Goes to Cleveland to Lecture," *Cincinnati Enquirer,* December 17, 1934; "Hundredth Anniversary," *Cincinnati Enquirer,* April 3, 1935; "Miss Hinkle at the Mercantile," *Cincinnati Enquirer,* January 23, 1935; "Minutes," the Young Men's Mercantile Library Association, April 18, 1935.

11. Vitz, *At the Center,* 111.

CHAPTER 5: READERS AND PUBLISHERS

1. John H. Westerhoff, *McGuffey and His Readers; Piety, Morality, and Education in Nineteenth-Century America* (Nashville: Abingdon, 1978), 14; John Clubbe, *Cincinnati Observed: Architecture and History* (Columbus: Ohio State University Press, 1992), 139.

2. Melancthon Tope, *A Biography of William Holmes McGuffey* (Bowerston, OH: Phrenological Era Print., 1929), 11.

3. Mauck Brammer, "Winthrop B. Smith: Creator of the Eclectic Educational Series," *Ohio History* 80 (1971): 48–50.

4. "McGuffey and His Readers," http://spec.lib.muohio.edu/; "William Holmes McGuffey Museum," http://www.units.muohio.edu/mcguffeymuseum/.

5. Henry Hobart Vail, *A History of the McGuffey Readers* (Cleveland: Burrows Brothers, 1911), 26.

6. William E. Smith, *About the McGuffeys: William Holmes McGuffey and Alexander H. McGuffey* (Oxford, OH: Typoprint, 1967), 12.

7. Stanley W. Lindberg, preface to *The Annotated McGuffey: Selections from the McGuffey Eclectic Readers, 1836–1920,* ed. Stanley W. Lindberg (New York: Van Nostrand Reinhold, 1976).

8. Westerhoff, *McGuffey and His Readers*, 53; Vail, *History of the McGuffey Readers*, 8, 29.

9. Woodward had once been a high school, and later became one again. Harvey C. Minnich, *William Holmes McGuffey and His Readers* (New York: American Book Company, 1936), 154.

10. Alexander McGuffey lived at 300 Southern Avenue in a frame house with a small front portico, matching gable roof, and several side porches and balconies. He died in the house in 1896. *Cincinnati: A Guide to the Queen City and Its Neighbors* (Cincinnati: Wiesen-Hart Press, 1943), 365; Smith, *About the McGuffeys*, 17.

11. Lindberg, preface to *Annotated McGuffey*, xix–xx.

12. Smith, *About the McGuffeys*, 15–18; "Book Review: William Holmes McGuffey," http://www.historyliteracy.org/scripts/search_display.php?Article_ID=84. The William Holmes McGuffey Museum in Oxford has a portrait of Caroline Virginia Rich McGuffey by Thomas Buchanan Read.

13. Lindberg, preface to *Annotated McGuffey*, xix.

14. Truman and Smith is listed in the 1834 *Deming Cincinnati City Directory* as located at what was then 150 Main Street. Truman boarded at S. Woodbury's on Baker Street and is listed as treasurer of the Young Men's Temperance Society. Brammer, "Winthrop B. Smith," 45–47, 53.

15. Smith, *About the McGuffeys*, 9; Westerhoff, *McGuffey and His Readers*, 54–55.

16. Lindberg, preface to *Annotated McGuffey*, xxi.

17. Vail, *History of the McGuffey Readers*, 34–35; Brammer, "Winthrop B. Smith," 51 and 53; Lindberg, *Annotated McGuffey*, xix.

18. "Says McGuffey Readers Made 10 Cincinnatians Millionaires . . . ," *Cincinnati Times-Star*, July 27, 1936, 1.

19. Lindberg, preface to *Annotated McGuffey*, xix–xx, xxii.

20. Brammer, "Winthrop B. Smith," 54, 54n26.

21. Minnich, *William Holmes McGuffey*, 40, 87; "American Book Company Records," http://library.syr.edu/digital/guides/a/amer_book_co.htm.

22. Clubbe, *Cincinnati Observed*, 139.

CHAPTER 6: A POEM IN THE PICTURE

1. John R. Tait, "Reminiscences of a Poet-Painter," *Lippincott's Magazine* 19 (1877): 307–308. The information about Cyrus Garrett is from the 1853 *Williams' City Directory*, 139. Garrett's firm was Garrett and Cottman at 9 West Seventh Street. He lived at what was then 68 West Eighth Street, later 21 East Eighth Street.

2. Robert C. Vitz, *The Queen and the Arts: Cultural Life in Nineteenth-Century Cincinnati* (Kent: Kent State University Press, 1989), 28.

3. "Obituary: Thomas Buchanan Read," *New York Times*, May 12, 1872; William H. Venable and Gene D. Lewis, "Personal Recollections of Thomas Buchanan Read," *Cincinnati Historical Society Bulletin* 23, no. 4 (1965): 282–84.

4. Venable and Lewis, "Personal Recollections," 280–81.

5. Dale Patrick Brown, *Brilliance and Balderdash: Early Lectures at Cincinnati's Mercantile Library* (Cincinnati: Mercantile Library, 2007), 61; Tait, "Reminiscences of a Poet-Painter," 320.

6. Vitz, *Queen and the Arts*, 178.

7. Venable and Lewis, "Personal Recollections," 279–80.

8. Henry Clay Townsend, *A Memoir of T. Buchanan Read* (Philadelphia, 1889), 17; Harvey S. Ford, "Thomas Buchanan Read and the Civil War: The Story of Sheridan's Ride," *Ohio History* 56, no. 3 (1947): 217.

9. The poem was actually entitled "The Oath." Ford, "Thomas Buchanan Read," 218.

10. Ibid., 218–21.

11. Henry Dudley Teetor, "Origins of Sheridan's Ride," *Magazine of Western History* 11 (1890): 567.

12. There are various accounts of the writing of the poem, and some suggest that Murdoch rather than Garrett proposed the poem to Read. Ford, "Thomas Buchanan Read," 224–25; "The Murdoch Testimonial Last Night," *Cincinnati Daily Commercial*, November 1, 1864, 2.

13. John Fleischman, "The Object at Hand," http://smithsonianmag .com/history-archaeology/object_nov96.html, 2.

14. Burnet House was on the northwest corner of Third and Vine. William Dudley Foulke, *Life of Oliver P. Morton, Including His Important Speeches*, 2 vols. (Kansas City: Bowen-Merrill, 1899), 1:191–92.

15. The poem is said to have appeared in the *Cincinnati Daily Commercial* for New Year's Day, 1868, but it cannot be located on that date or on New Year's Day, 1867, when the bridge opened to the public. Venable and Lewis, "Personal Recollections," 280.

16. Tait, "Reminiscences of a Poet-Painter," 321.

17. "Obituary: Thomas Buchanan Read."

18. The Literary Club of Cincinnati, which was located next door from 1896 to 1930, provided the marker.

CHAPTER 7: THE POET SISTERS

1. Unless otherwise specified, the information in this chapter is taken from the author's June 2009 tour of Cary Cottage or from Mary Clemmer Ames, *A Memorial of Alice and Phoebe Cary, with Some of Their Later Poems* (New York: Hurd and Houghton, 1873).

2. Typhoid is listed as the cause of death in burial records at Cincinnati's Spring Grove Cemetery.

3. Judith Fetterley, introduction to Alice Cary, *Clovernook Sketches and Other Stories,* ed. Judith Fetterley (New Brunswick: Rutgers University Press, 1987), xv.

4. Ibid., xvi, xx.

5. Ibid., xvi; Edgar Allan Poe, review of Rufus Wilmot Griswold, *The Female Poets of America, Southern Literary Messenger* (February 1849): 126–27, http://www.eapoe.org/works/criticsm/slm49g01.htm.

6. Fetterley, introduction to Cary, *Clovernook Sketches,* xx. The information about *Hagar* is from Ames, *Memorial,* 35.

7. "The Cary Sisters," http://www25.uua.org/uuhs/duub/articles /carysisters.html.

8. "The Cary Sisters' Old Home," *New York Times,* June 30, 1881.

CHAPTER 8: THE FATHER OF THE QUEEN

1. "University of Cincinnati, OMI College of Applied Science Timeline," http://www.omicas175.uc.edu/histtimelinfo.asp; Henry Wadsworth Longfellow, *The Poetical Works of Longfellow* (Boston: Houghton Mifflin, 1975), 196.

2. The portrait, which is by Robert S. Duncanson, is on long-term loan from the owner, the University of Cincinnati.

3. John Clubbe, *Cincinnati Observed: Architecture and History* (Columbus: Ohio State University Press, 1992), 143.

4. Ibid.

5. "The Late Nicholas Longworth," http://www.sonofthesouth.net /leefoundation/civil-war/1863/nicholas-longworth.htm.

6. Longworth was important for other reasons. He is sometimes described as the man who brought art to the West. He was one of the founders of the Cincinnati Academy of Fine Arts and was noteworthy for his patronage of artists who became famous, among them the sculptor Hiram Powers, America's first major female painter, Lily Martin Spencer, and painter/poet Thomas Buchanan Read. Longworth was a staunch opponent of slavery, and, with his help, the African American painter Robert Duncanson became one of the finest landscape painters in the country. Longworth was also a major philanthropist. See Clubbe, *Cincinnati Observed,* 143; "Nicholas Longworth: Father of the American Wine Industry," http://www.weekendwinery.com /wineryinsight/Article_Jul03.htm.

7. Peter Bronson, "Longworth Put Poetry in a Bottle," *Cincinnati Enquirer,* May 17, 2009.

8. Sparks was president of Harvard from 1849 to 1853. Samuel Longfellow, *Life of Henry Wadsworth Longfellow,* 2 vols. (Boston: Ticknor, 1886), 1:349.

9. Michael Teague, *Mrs. L.: Conversations with Alice Roosevelt Longworth* (Garden City, NY: Doubleday, 1981), 137. The information about the rooks appears on the caption for a carved mantel from Rookwood on display at the Cincinnati Art Museum.

10. Geoffrey J. Giglierano and Deborah A. Overmyer, *The Bicentennial Guide to Greater Cincinnati: A Portrait of Two Hundred Years* (Cincinnati: Cincinnati Historical Society, 1988), 359; Clara Longworth Chambrun, *The Making of Nicholas Longworth* (New York: Bramwell Press, 1933), 53–59; Gamaliel Bailey Jr., *American Progress* (Cincinnati: Edwin Shepard, 1846); *Annual Report,* Young Men's Library Association (Cincinnati: Young Men's Mercantile Library Association, 1846), 17.

11. The poet apparently rejected the idea, but Powers eventually completed such a sculpture in Europe in the late 1860s. Nicholas Longworth to Longfellow, December 15, 1851, and January 30, 1852. By permission of the Houghton Library, Harvard University. Call number bMS Am 1340.2 (3528).

12. Joseph Longworth to Longfellow, June 1, 1854. By permission of the Houghton Library, Harvard University. Call number bMS Am 1340.2 (3527).

13. Joseph's daughter was Maria Longworth Nichols Storer, founder of the famous Rookwood pottery, which she named after her father's home. Joseph's grandson was Nicholas III, who became U.S. speaker of the House. Nicholas III married Teddy Roosevelt's daughter Alice in a well-publicized White House wedding. *Annual Report,* the Young Men's Mercantile Library Association (Cincinnati: Young Men's Mercantile Library Association, 1890), 9.

14. In a list of the holdings of Harvard University's Houghton Library, there is a copy of *The Song of Hiawatha,* autographed to Joseph in November 1855. Henry Wadsworth Longfellow, *The Letters of Henry Wadsworth Longfellow,* 6 vols. (Cambridge: Belknap Press of Harvard University Press, 1966–82), 3:494.

15. In November of 1855, Longfellow sent the pebble to Thomas Gold Appleton, noting that he had received "a very pretty painting on canvas;— a charming group of trees, and a poetic cloud-sky" from the Longworths. "You will like it," he said. Joseph Longworth to Longfellow, October 20, 1855. By permission of the Houghton Library, Harvard University. Call number bMS Am 1340.2 (3527).

16. Joseph Longworth to Longfellow, February 11, 1858. By permission of the Houghton Library, Harvard University. Call number bMS Am 1340.2 (3527).

17. Longfellow, *Letters,* 4:486.

18. Chambrun, *Making of Nicholas Longworth,* 33–34.

19. Joseph Longworth to Longfellow, September 11, 1865. By permission of the Houghton Library, Harvard University. Call number bMS Am 1340.2 (3527).

20. Several Mercantile annual reports, including those of 1870 and 1871, list Joseph Longworth as a life member. Judge Nicholas Longworth II was

also a life member. "Cornelia & all her jewels," puzzling for modern readers, refers to the Roman matron Cornelia, the classical ideal of the wife and mother. Longworth to Longfellow, November 19, 1855. By permission of the Houghton Library, Harvard University. Call number bMS Am 1340.2 (3527).

21. Anita Israel, telephone interview by author, January 20, 2005; Samuel Longfellow, *Life of Henry Wadsworth Longfellow,* vol. 2; Fanny Appleton Longfellow, *Mrs. Longfellow: Selected Letters and Journals of Fanny Appleton Longfellow (1817–1851),* ed. Edward Wagenknecht (New York: Longmans, Green, 1956), 203; Thomas Wentworth Higginson, *Henry Wadsworth Longfellow* (Boston: Houghton Mifflin, 1902), 204.

CHAPTER 9: TWO TALES OF A CITY

1. "The Dickens Trail," *Cincinnati Post,* May 4, 1940, 9.

2. "Tiresome, Boring Citizenry," *Cincinnati Post,* February 20, 1934, 18; Robert Price, "Boz Reports on Ohio," *Ohio History* 51, no. 3 (1942): 197.

3. John Forster, *The Life of Charles Dickens,* 3 vols. (Philadelphia: J. B. Lippincott, 1872), 1:379–80.

4. Gordon A. Christenson, "A Tale of Two Lawyers in Antebellum Cincinnati: Timothy Walker's Last Interview with Salmon P. Chase," *University of Cincinnati Law Review* 71 (2002): 457–91.

5. Alfred R. Ferguson, "Charles Dickens in Ohio," *Ohio History* 59, no. 1 (1950): 14–25; Christenson, "Tale of Two Lawyers," 457.

6. "Dickens Trail."

7. Hewson L. Peeke, "Charles Dickens in Ohio in 1842," *Ohio History* 28, no. 1 (1919): 73.

8. Walker liked Dickens too. In his journal entry for April 5, 1842, he mentioned the tour of the city and the party he gave for Dickens. "Have read all his works over with great interest," he said. "Felt acquainted with him before I saw him. Like him still better now." The journal is in the Timothy Walker Papers at the Cincinnati Historical Society. Price, "Boz Reports on Ohio," 198; Christenson, "Tale of Two Lawyers," 483.

9. Charles Dickens, *American Notes* (Greenwich, CT: Fawcett, 1961), 189–90; "Tiresome, Boring Citizenry," *Cincinnati Post,* February 20, 1934, 18; The letters were originally published in Forster, *Life of Charles Dickens,* vol. 1.

10. Peeke, "Charles Dickens in Ohio," 72–75.

11. Dickens to Timothy Walker, Niagara Falls, April 30, 1842.

CHAPTER 10: ONES COMING WITH PAPERS

1. J. Roger Newstedt, introduction to *The Literary Club of Cincinnati, 1849–1999* (Cincinnati: Literary Club of Cincinnati, 2001), xi–xiv.

2. "*Life* Visits the Cincinnati Literary Club," *Life*, March 26, 1951, 149–55.

3. Mary K. Cayton, "The Making of an American Prophet," *American Historical Review* 92 (1987): 607–20; "Lectures on the Nineteenth Century," *Cincinnati Daily Times,* May 18, 1850.

4. The financial arrangements and the profits are reported in "The Introduction to the Edition of 1890," reprinted in *The Literary Club of Cincinnati, 1849–1903* (Cincinnati: Ebbert and Richardson, 1903), 15.

5. "Diary and Letters of Rutherford B. Hayes," http://www.ohiohistory .org/onlinedoc/hayes/volume01/Chapter09/SundayMay26.txt.

6. "Introduction to the Edition of 1890," 15–16.

7. John A. Diehl, "The Club Historian's 159th Anniversary Address: The Celestial Branch," in *Literary Club of Cincinnati, 1849–1999,* 16.

8. Eslie Asbury, "The Literary Club," in *The Literary Club Papers of Eslie Asbury,* vol. 1 (Cincinnati: Literary Club of Cincinnati, 1970), ix.

9. Ibid., xii.

10. James Albert Green, "The Hundred Years," in *The Literary Club of Cincinnati, 1849–1949* (Cincinnati: Roessler Bros., 1949), 31; Asbury, "Physicians of the Literary Club, 1849–1966," in *Literary Club Papers of Eslie Asbury,* 178.

11. David Reichert, "The History and Lore of the Club," in *Literary Club of Cincinnati, 1849–1999,* 29–30. Hayes's writing for the club is mentioned in Henry Winkler's "One Hundred Fifty Years Young," which also appears in *Literary Club of Cincinnati, 1849–1999,* 22.

12. "Diary and Letters of Rutherford B. Hayes," http://www.ohiohistory .org/onlinedoc/hayes/chapterxxxvi.html.

13. Winkler, "One Hundred Fifty Years Young," 22; Reichert, "History and Lore of the Club," 30.

14. Eslie Asbury, "Literary Club," viii, and "Physicians of the Literary Club, 1849–1966," in *Literary Club Papers of Eslie Asbury,* 177.

15. Ed F. Alexander, "500 East Fourth Street," and Reichert, "History and Lore of the Club," in *Literary Club of Cincinnati, 1849–1999,* 87 and 33, respectively.

16. Winkler, "One Hundred Fifty Years Young," 26.

17. Noon Day meets in the homes of members once a month from October to June. Papers written by members are read on a rotating basis.

18. Eslie Asbury, "For but Off the Record" in *Literary Club Papers of Eslie Asbury,* 79; Asbury, "Literary Club," vii.

19. Eslie Asbury, "108th Anniversary," in *Literary Club Papers of Eslie Asbury,* 122.

20. Newstedt, introduction to *Literary Club of Cincinnati, 1849–1999,* xiii–xiv; Asbury, "Literary Club," xii.

21. "*Life* Visits the Cincinnati Literary Club," 149.

22. Eslie Asbury, "A Letter to the Editor," in *Literary Club Papers of Eslie Asbury*, 158.

23. Reichert, "History and Lore of the Club," 34.

CHAPTER II: J. B. POND'S SERVANT

1. William Baker, "Mark Twain in Cincinnati: A Mystery Most Compelling," *American Literary Realism* 12, no. 2 (1979): 299–315.

2. Ibid.; Albert Bigelow Paine, *Mark Twain: A Biography*, 3 vols. (New York: Harper and Brothers, 1912), 1:112–15.

3. Baker, "Mark Twain in Cincinnati," 303–4.

4. Ibid., 305–8.

5. This would have been on the south side of Third, between Race and Elm, on a slope of Fort Washington Way. The Walnut Street address was covered by Riverfront Stadium and is now approximately where the Underground Railroad Freedom Center is located. *Williams' City Directory, City Guide and Business Mirror* (Cincinnati: C. S. Williams, 1857); Baker, "Mark Twain in Cincinnati," 302.

6. The Odeon, which was located at Elm and Grant adjacent to Music Hall, is listed as the location of the event on a ticket in the holdings of the Public Library of Cincinnati and Hamilton County. "Twain and Cable," *Cincinnati Enquirer*, January 3, 1885.

7. Ibid.; "Another Delighted Audience," *Cincinnati Enquirer*, January 4, 1885.

8. "Twain and Cable."

9. Ibid.

10. Eslie Asbury, "Rare Moments in Club History," in *The Literary Club Papers of Eslie Asbury*, vol. 1 (Cincinnati: Literary Club of Cincinnati, 1970), 231.

CHAPTER 12: THE DEAN AND THE QUEEN

1. William Dean Howells, *Years of My Youth, and Three Essays* (Bloomington: Indiana University Press, 1975), 127–39. The pseudonyms are described in Susan Goodman, *William Dean Howells: A Writer's Life* (Berkeley: University of California Press, 2005), 32, and William Dean Howells, *My Literary Passions* (New York: Harper, 1895), 39.

2. Howells, *Years of My Youth*, 140.

3. Goodman, *William Dean Howells*, 33.

4. One of them was the *New England No. 2*, a steamboat built in 1848. Howells, *Years of My Youth*, 10–30.

5. F. C. Marston Jr., "An Early Howells Letter," *American Literature* 18 (1946): 163–64.

6. Howells, *My Literary Passions*, 165.

7. Howells, *Years of My Youth*, 141.

8. Ibid., 142–44, 154.

9. Goodman, *William Dean Howells*, 41.

10. This period is thoroughly covered by Robert Price in "The Road to Boston: 1860 Travel Correspondence of William Dean Howells," *Ohio History* 80 (1971): 85–154. According to Price, Howells was annoyed that the *Gazette* didn't publish everything he sent them. However, the *Gazette* did publish at least seven thousand words from the trip, and the columns flow smoothly. Most likely, as Price speculates, it was poems that the *Gazette* rejected, and perhaps with good reason.

11. Ibid., 126.

12. See W. D. Howells, Mark Twain, Nathaniel S. Shaler, and Others, *The Niagara Book* (New York: Doubleday, Page, 1901).

13. Price, "Road to Boston," 89–90.

14. Howells, *Years of My Youth*, 74.

15. "John James Piatt," http://famousamericans.net/johnjamespiatt/.

16. Clara M. Kirk and Rudolf Kirk, *William Dean Howells* (New York: Twayne, 1962), 42.

17. William D. Baker, *William Dean Howells: The Influence of Ohio on His Life and Works* (Columbus: State Library of Ohio, 1979), 12. Howells and his wife visited Hayes in the White House when he became president.

18. Kirk, *William Dean Howells*, 51.

19. Goodman, *William Dean Howells*, 11.

20. David D. Anderson, *Ohio: In Fact and Fiction: Further Essays on the Ohio Experience* (East Lansing: Midwestern Press, Center for the Study of Midwestern Literature and Culture, Michigan State University, 2006), 48.

21. Baker, *William Dean Howells*, 1, 22n1. The letter to the principal is in the Peaslee Papers of the Ohio Historical Society.

22. Anderson, *Ohio*, 62.

23. Robert Rowlette, "William D. Howells' Midwest Lecture Tour," *American Literary Realism, 1870–1910* 10, no. 2 (1977): 146–48.

CHAPTER 13: A HAIRDRESSER TELLING ALL

1. "Revelations of a Fashionable Hair-Dresser," *Cincinnati Daily Gazette*, October 19, 1859, 2.

2. "A Reviewer Reviewed," *Cincinnati Daily Commercial*, October 20, 1859, 2.

3. Eliza Potter, *A Hairdresser's Experience in High Life* (New York: Oxford University Press, 1991), 71, 204, 293.

4. Ibid., 159.

5. Ibid., 178.

6. Ibid., 233–34, 260–61.

7. Ibid., 30, 91, 286–90.

8. The 1860 U.S. Census for the city of Cincinnati lists Eliza Potter as forty years old, born about 1820 in New York. However, the 1860 Census for Niagara, New York, taken a few months later, lists her as born in Virginia. It seems likely that she lied about her age, because otherwise she would have been impossibly young for some of the events she describes. For the best available biographical information and commentary, see the edition of *A Hairdresser's Experience in High Life* edited by Xiomara Santamarina (Chapel Hill: University of North Carolina Press, 2009).

9. Potter, *Hairdresser's Experience* (1991), 11–12 and 20.

10. "Revelations."

11. Santamarina, introduction to Potter, *Hairdresser's Experience* (2009), xiv.

12. Potter, *Hairdresser's Experience* (1991), 27, 196.

13. Louisa A. Taylor is the young hairdresser listed at Potter's address in the 1860 U.S. Census for the city of Cincinnati.

14. According to Santamarina, Eliza and Howard Potter were married on December 8, 1853. See Santamarina, introduction to *Hairdresser's Experience* (2009), xv. The children and their ages are from the 1860 U.S. Census for the city of Cincinnati.

15. Home Street is a small street, now more like an alley, between Elm and Plum. It runs north between Fourth and Fifth and is near the current Duke Energy Convention Center. The financial information is from the 1860 U.S. census for the city of Cincinnati.

16. Potter, *Hairdresser's Experience* (1991), 18. According to Santamarina (201n11), this is a biblical reference to a period of peace and prosperity.

17. Nikki M. Taylor, *Frontiers of Freedom: Cincinnati's Black Community, 1802–1868* (Athens: Ohio University Press, 2005), 136.

18. U.S. Census Bureau, *Population of the United States in 1860* (Washington, DC: Government Printing Office, 1864) .

19. Potter, *Hairdresser's Experience* (1991), 16–19. Santamarina dates this episode to 1834, although detailed information is still missing. Introduction to Potter, *Hairdresser's Experience* (2009), xvi.

20. Potter, *Hairdresser's Experience* (1991), 196.

21. Ibid., 19, 74, 276–77.

22. Ibid., III, IV.

23. Ibid., 97–102, 110.

24. Ibid., 67, 281–82.

25. Sharon G. Dean, introduction to Potter, *Hairdresser's Experience* (1991), l.

26. Potter, *Hairdresser's Experience* (1991), 68.

27. Dean, introduction to Potter, *Hairdresser's Experience* (1991), xlviii.

28. Xiomara Santamarina, "Black Hairdresser and Social Critic: Eliza Potter and the Labors of Femininity," *American Literature* 77, no. 1 (2005): 152, 156.

29. Potter, *Hairdresser's Experience* (1991), 212.

30. Santamarina, introduction to Potter, *Hairdresser's Experience* (2009), xv, and 1860 U.S. Census for Niagara, New York, 1860.

31. Santamarina, app. A to Potter, *Hairdresser's Experience* (2009).

32. The other "voices" in the presentation, available online through the catalogue of the Public Library of Cincinnati and Hamilton County, are Frances Trollope and riverboat captain James S. Wise.

CHAPTER 14: THE NEW JOURNALIST

1. George M. Gould, *Concerning Lafcadio Hearn* (Philadelphia: George W. Jacobs, 1908), 3. According to Vitz and several other sources, Hearn arrived in Cincinnati in 1869. Robert C. Vitz, *The Queen and the Arts: Cultural Life in Nineteenth-Century Cincinnati* (Kent: Kent State University Press, 1989). Gould says 1870, and some writers say as late as 1871.

2. Vitz, *Queen and the Arts,* 133.

3. Nina H. Kennard, *Lafcadio Hearn* (New York: D. Appleton, 1912), 48, 73; "Lafcadio Hearn," http://www.britannica.com/EBchecked/topic /258314/Lafcadio-Hearn.

4. Kennard, *Lafcadio Hearn,* 74–75; Graydon DeCamp, *The Grand Old Lady of Vine Street* (Cincinnati: Cincinnati Enquirer, 1991), 64.

5. Lafcadio Hearn, preface to *Articles on Literature and Other Writings from the Cincinnati Enquirer, 1873* (New York: AMS Press, 1975), 2.

6. Kennard, *Lafcadio Hearn,* 75.

7. Tom Wolfe, *The New Journalism* (New York: Harper and Row, 1973), 31–33, 45–46.

8. Kennard, *Lafcadio Hearn,* 79.

9. Steve Kemme, "Cincinnati Shaped His Style," *Cincinnati Enquirer,* September 20, 2004; DeCamp, *Grand Old Lady of Vine Street,* 64; Vitz, *Queen and the Arts,* 135; Kennard, *Lafcadio Hearn,* 73.

10. Kennard, *Lafcadio Hearn,* 78–79.

11. "Cincinnati Shaped His Style."

12. Vera McWilliams, *Lafcadio Hearn* (Boston: Houghton Mifflin, 1946), 81.

13. John Clubbe, *Cincinnati Observed: Architecture and History* (Columbus: Ohio State University Press, 1992), 14.

14. Clement J. Barnhorn, "Cincinnati Studios Lafcadio Hearn Knew," photo, *Cincinnati Enquirer,* June 8, 1930, Mag 3.

15. Gould, *Concerning Lafcadio Hearn,* 20; DeCamp, *Grand Old Lady of Vine Street,* 65.

16. Gould, *Concerning Lafcadio Hearn,* 21.

17. Jon Christopher Hughes, *The Tanyard Murder: On the Case with Lafcadio Hearn* (Washington: University Press of America, 1982), xv–xvi.

18. DeCamp, *Grand Old Lady of Vine Street,* 64–65. His last article, "The Sub-Worthington Suit," is mentioned in Hearn, preface to *Articles on Literature,* 2.

19. When Hearn died, Mattie sued his estate for a widow's interest, claiming she left him because of his "morose and moody temperament" but that they had never legally divorced. Apparently, they were never legally married either. The courts ruled their marriage illegal because state laws prohibited marriage between the races. See "Widow of Lafcadio Hearn?" *New York Times,* July 14, 1906, and Kennard, *Lafcadio Hearn,* 83.

20. DeCamp, *Grand Old Lady of Vine Street,* 65–66.

21. Kennard, *Lafcadio Hearn,* 88–91; Gould, *Concerning Lafcadio Hearn,* 38; McWilliams, *Lafcadio Hearn,* 98.

22. Kennard, *Lafcadio Hearn,* 73.

23. See Lafcadio Hearn, *Letters from the Raven* (New York: Albert and Charles Boni, 1930).

24. Ibid., 85–86, 105.

25. "Cincinnati Shaped His Style."

26. Main Library—Special Collections—The Lafcadio Hearn Collection, http://www.cincinnatilibrary.org/main/hearn.html; Alfred Kleine-Kreutzmann, "The Development of the Lafcadio Hearn Collection at the Public Library of Cincinnati and Hamilton County," in *Centennial Essays on Lafcadio Hearn,* edited by Kenji Zenimoto (Matsue, Japan: Hearn Society, 1996), 286.

27. John Fleischman, *Free and Public* (Wilmington, OH: Orange Frazer Press, 2003), 76.

CHAPTER 15: A GOOD ONE

1. Biographical details of Hurst's early years are readily available on the website of Brandeis University, which holds a large Fannie Hurst Collection: http://lts.brandeis.edu/research/archives-speccoll/findingguides/xml/hurst.html#doe99. However, the site lists her birth year as 1889, and it is more likely 1885.

2. Fannie Hurst, *Anatomy of Me: A Wonderer in Search of Herself* (Garden City, NY: Doubleday, 1958), 30.

3. Fannie Hurst, *Back Street* (New York: Cosmopolitan Book, 1931), 3.

4. Brooke Kroeger, *Fannie: The Talent for Success of Writer Fannie Hurst* (New York: Times Books, 1999), 275–76.

5. Hurst, *Anatomy of Me,* 6

6. Ibid., 32–36.

7. Ibid., 3.

8. Kroeger, *Fannie,* 7, 15, 19.

9. Ibid., 341, 344.

10. Ibid., 12.

11. *Back Street* was the first sound movie filmed in Cincinnati, according to Nick Clooney, "Back Street First Talkie Filmed Here," *Cincinnati Post,* June 11, 2003.

12. "Cincinnati Book Locale Fannie Hurst Tells Why She Uses City as Basis of Novel," *Cincinnati Enquirer,* January 31, 1931, 6.

13. "Fannie Hurst Visits Here," *Cincinnati Enquirer,* November 9, 1965, 8.

14. "Fannie Hurst Will Visit Here in September," *Cincinnati Post,* August 24, 1928, 11;. "Beneficiaries Include Fannie Hurst," *Cincinnati Enquirer,* March 5, 1940, 24. William Frieder was Aunt Jennie's second husband. Her first husband, Joe, died in 1925.

15. "Female Status Has Changed," *Cincinnati Enquirer,* October 26, 1932, 16.

16. "Sentimental Journey," *Cincinnati Times-Star,* May 9, 1955, 1.

17. "Sentimental Journey," *Cincinnati Post,* May 9, 1955, 20.

18. Fannie Hurst Collection.

19. "Fannie Hurst Wed; Hid Secret 5 Years," *New York Times,* May 4, 1920.

20. Kroeger, *Fannie,* 345.

21. She bequeathed one million dollars to Brandeis and Washington Universities to establish professorships in creative writing. http://www.jewishvirtuallibrary.org/jsource/biography/hurst.html. She is buried in St. Louis with her parents.

22. "Fannie Hurst," *New York Times,* July 27, 2009.

CHAPTER 16: HERETIC AT CINCINNATI

1. Lawrance Roger Thompson, *Robert Frost: A Biography* (New York: Holt, Rinehart and Winston, 1981), 18.

2. "In Society," *Cincinnati Enquirer,* January 12, 1922.

3. Mrs. Louise Reichert, interview by author, Cincinnati, June 11, 2003; Luella Nash LeVee, "A Tribute to Robert Frost," *Cincinnati Enquirer,* March 24, 1974, 10. Unless otherwise indicated, subsequent information regarding Frost and the Reicherts is from the interview with Mrs. Reichert. Mrs. Reichert is now deceased.

4. "Noted Poet Says Verse Writers Have Best Chance for Posterity," *Cincinnati Times-Star,* November 2, 1938, 9; interview with Mrs. Louise Reichert.

5. For biographical details, see Jay Parini, *Robert Frost: A Life* (New York: Henry Holt, 1999).

6. Andrew R. Marks, *The Rabbi and the Poet: Victor Reichert and Robert Frost* (Alton, NH: Andover Green, 1994), 8–9.

7. "Famous Poet No Longer Feels Badly . . . ," *Cincinnati Post,* April 17, 1944, 14.

8. Raymond Walters, journal, April 19, 1944, University of Cincinnati Library.

9. Luella Nash LeVee, telephone interview by author, June 13, 2003; "Tribute to Robert Frost."

10. "Frost to Read His Poems at UC This Afternoon," *Cincinnati Enquirer,* October 9, 1946, 3.

11. Victor Reichert, "Sense of Value Is Passed . . . ," *Cincinnati Enquirer,* November 1, 1959, 1j.

12. Ibid.

13. Victor E. Reichert, "What, That Atheist," in *A Literary Club Sampler: 1939–1992* (Cincinnati: Literary Club of Cincinnati, 1993), 287.

14. Thompson, *Robert Frost,* 38.

15. "UC to Confer Top Honor on Robert Frost Tonight," *Cincinnati Post,* November 15, 1954, 8.

16. David Reichert, telephone interview by author, June 13, 2003.

17. Ibid.

18. "Honored Guest," *Cincinnati Enquirer,* November 1, 1954, 4; "Students Meet Robert Frost . . . ," *Cincinnati Post,* November 19, 1954, 21.

19. Marks, *Rabbi and The Poet,* 24.

20. Reichert, "What, That Atheist," 292.

21. Eslie Asbury, MD, "The Literary Club," *Filson Club History Quarterly* 44, no. 3 (1970): 222–23.

22. Marks, *Rabbi and the Poet,* 48.

CHAPTER 17: BABBITTRY

1. Lewis was in Cincinnati by February 16, 1921, at the latest. See Sinclair Lewis to Lowman Lewis, February 16, 1921, Sinclair Lewis Collection, Port Washington Public Library.

2. Carl Van Doren, *Sinclair Lewis: A Biographical Sketch* (Garden City, NY: Doubleday, Doran, 1933), 74.

3. James Albert Green, *Sketch of the History of the Queen City Club: 1874–1934* (Cincinnati: Queen City Club, 1934), 9.

4. John Clubbe, *Cincinnati Observed: Architecture and History* (Columbus: Ohio State University Press, 1992), 130; Geoffrey J. Giglierano and Deborah A. Overmyer, *The Bicentennial Guide to Greater Cincinnati: A Portrait of Two Hundred Years* (Cincinnati: Cincinnati Historical Society, 1988), 60.

5. Sinclair Lewis to Rupert Hughes, March 1, 1921, Sinclair Lewis Collection, Port Washington Public Library. In order to stay at the Queen City

Club, Lewis would have had to be introduced by a member who took responsibility for him during his stay.

6. James M. Hutchisson, "'All of Us Americans at 46': The Making of Sinclair Lewis' *Babbitt*," in *George F. Babbitt*, ed. Harold Bloom (Philadelphia: Chelsea House, 2004), 90.

7. Ibid., 90–91.

8. Sinclair Lewis, *Babbitt* (San Diego: Harcourt, Brace, 1922), 221, 312, 415.

9. "Pogue's Take Pleasure in Announcing . . . ," *Cincinnati Commercial*, March 7, 1921, 7.

10. "Famous Novelist Criticizes Famous Evangelist . . . ," *Cincinnati Post*, March 10, 1921, 2.

11. Richard R. Lingeman, *Sinclair Lewis: Rebel from Main Street* (New York: Random House, 2002), 164.

12. Helen Batchelor, "A Sinclair Lewis Portfolio of Maps: Zenith to Winnemac," *Modern Language Quarterly* 32 (1971): 401–8.

13. Lingeman, *Sinclair Lewis*, 397.

14. Bob Richards, "Lewis Says He'll Retire when 80," *Cincinnati Post*, February 17, 1938, 22.

15. James T. Golden Jr., "Sinclair Lewis Talks on Books . . . ," *Cincinnati Enquirer*, February 18, 1938. He divorced his first wife, Grace, and eventually divorced Dorothy as well.

16. "Epigram-Studded Lecture Heard by Business Men," *Cincinnati Times-Star*, February 18, 1938, 10.

17. *The Cincinnati Woman's Club: Historical Sketch in Honor of the 75th Anniversary of the Founding of the Club: 1894–1969* (Cincinnati: The Club, 1969), 56.

18. "Rotary Club Forgives Caustic References," *Cincinnati Times-Star*, November 21, 1941, 27.

19. "Late Novelist Visited City," *Cincinnati Times-Star*, January 11, 1951, 22.

20. "Debaters Agree Jap War Ends Danger of Fascism," *Cincinnati Times-Star*, December 10, 1941, 10.

CHAPTER 18: THE POET LAUREATE OF GREETING CARDS

1. "Obituaries," *Cincinnati Enquirer*, April 25, 1981, D1.

2. "Celebrity Status Amazes Poet," *Cincinnati Enquirer*, April 3, 1980, E1; Ronald Pollitt, *Helen Steiner Rice: Ambassador of Sunshine* (Grand Rapids, MI: F. H. Revell, 1994), 17–20.

3. Helen Steiner Rice, *In the Vineyard of the Lord* (Old Tappan, NJ: F. H. Revell, 1979), 16.

4. Ibid., 28–37.

5. Pollitt, *Helen Steiner Rice*, 64–67.

6. "Celebrity Status Amazes Poet."

7. Pollitt, *Helen Steiner Rice*, 87–98, 112–14.

8. Laurie Petrie, "Poet Helen Rice Dies at Age 80," *Cincinnati Post,* April 24, 1981, 1a; Rice, *In the Vineyard of the Lord,* 65.

9. "Celebrity Status Amazes Poet."

10. Pollitt, *Helen Steiner Rice,* 143.

11. Rice, *In the Vineyard of the Lord,* 48–49.

12. Ibid., 69.

13. Pollitt, *Helen Steiner Rice,* 143.

14. "Celebrity Status Amazes Poet"; Rice, *In the Vineyard of the Lord,* 68.

15. Pollitt, *Helen Steiner Rice,* 121.

16. Ibid., 190.

17. "Poet Helen Rice Dies at Age 80."

18. Rice, *In the Vineyard of the Lord,* 79, 82.

19. Mary Wood, "Welk Again Reads Poem of Mrs. Rice," *Cincinnati Post Times-Star,* May 16, 1962, 42.

20. "Obituaries," *Cincinnati Enquirer,* April 25, 1981, D1.

21. Rice, *In the Vineyard of the Lord,* 98.

22. Pollitt, *Helen Steiner Rice,* 248–49, 262–64.

23. Ibid., 143.

24. "Steiner Rice, Ruthven Are Together Again," photo, *Cincinnati Enquirer,* June 15, 1997, E1.

25. "Celebrity Status Amazes Poet."

26. Pollitt, *Helen Steiner Rice,* 281–82.

27. "Obituaries."

CHAPTER 19: ANOTHER SPRING, ANOTHER POET

1. The photograph was described in a November 24, 2002, telephone interview by the author with Gilbert Bettman Jr., son of one of the participants. The date of the picnic, which was held at Ponderosa Ridge in Mount Airy Forest, is mentioned in the unpublished journal of the late Van Meter Ames, another participant, who was a University of Cincinnati philosophy professor. Copies of selected entries from the unpublished journal were generously provided by his daughter, Damaris Ames.

2. Iphigene Bettman, "A Miss of Contradictions," *Cincinnati Horizons* 3, no. 6 (1974): 24–28; Jeffrey R. Lueders, "George Elliston's Meeting Place for Poets," *Cincinnati Horizons* 11, no. 1 (1981): 31–33.

3. Iphigene Bettman, "A Miss of Contradictions," 26–28.

4. "Elliston Estate Is $250,000, Left for UC Poetry Fund," *Cincinnati Enquirer,* October 10, 1946.

5. Keith Stewart, interview by author, Cincinnati, December 16, 2002.

6. James V. Cummins, interview by author, Cincinnati, January 24, 2003. Cummins is a University of Cincinnati professor and curator of the Elliston Poetry Collection.

7. Interview with Gilbert Bettman Jr.; Bevis Hillier, *John Betjeman: New Fame, New Love* (London: John Murray, 2002), 578.

8. Interview with Stewart.

9. Raymond Walters, journal, February 8, 1951, University of Cincinnati Library.

10. John I. Ades, telephone interview by author, January 23, 2003. Dr. Ades was an instructor and graduate student at the University of Cincinnati during the period.

11. John Haffenden, *The Life of John Berryman* (Boston: Routledge and Kegan Paul, 1981), 225.

12. Paul Mariani, *Dream Song: The Life of John Berryman* (New York: W. Morrow, 1990), 24. The reference to Berryman's braces is from Valerie Foulkes, telephone interview by author, November 15, 2002. Ms. Foulkes was a member of the University of Cincinnati English faculty.

13. Hillier, *John Betjeman*, 578.

14. Pat Ford, telephone interview by author, November 18, 2002.

15. Ames, journal, March 30, 1952.

16. Haffenden, *Life of John Berryman*, 227.

17. Interview with Stewart.

18. Ames, journal, March 27, 1953.

19. Interview with Stewart.

20. Interview with Foulkes.

21. "Betjeman Wrote Impressions of City," *Cincinnati Enquirer*, April 13, 1957, 1.

22. Walter E. Langsam, interview by author, Cincinnati, January 17, 2003.

23. Interview with Stewart; "Walters Defends British Poet as Now Hostile to Reds," *Cincinnati Enquirer*, December 7, 1952, 27.

24. Stephen Spender, *Journals: 1939–1983* (New York: Random House, 1986), 122.

25. Betty Payne, telephone interview by author, November 22, 1992; Ames, journal, May 24, 1953. Ms. Payne was a curator of the Elliston Poetry Collection.

26. Ames, journal, March 25 and 27, 1954.

27. Interview with Gilbert Bettman Jr.

28. Ian Hamilton, *Robert Lowell: A Biography* (New York: Random House, 1982), 201–7; Paul Mariani, *Lost Puritan: A Life of Robert Lowell* (New York: W. W. Norton, 1994), 230–33.

29. Ames, journal, April 8, 1954.

30. Interview with Ford.

31. Interview with Gilbert Bettman Jr.

32. Hillier, *John Betjeman*, 572.

33. Hamilton, *Robert Lowell*, 209–10. The information concerning the cancellation of the last lecture came from Betty Payne.

34. Hamilton, *Robert Lowell*, 210–13.

35. Ibid., 210.

36. Interview with Stewart.

SELECTED BIBLIOGRAPHY

In the absence of a comprehensive book on Cincinnati's literary history since 1891, when W. H. Venable published his *Beginnings of Literary Culture in the Ohio Valley*, it has been necessary to fashion *Literary Cincinnati* from a particularly diverse assortment of sources, ranging from the traditional books, journal articles, and periodicals to annual reports, minute books, websites, unpublished correspondence, federal census records, city directories, and interviews conducted by the author. Significant pieces of information have also been gleaned from newspaper accounts only available on microfilm. Great care has been taken to document all sources in the footnotes, but, for the reader's convenience, some of the more substantive and readily available books and articles are listed here.

~

Ames, Mary Clemmer. *A Memorial of Alice and Phoebe Cary.* New York: Hurd and Houghton, 1873.

Asbury, Eslie. *The Literary Club Papers of Eslie Asbury.* Vol. 1. Cincinnati: Literary Club of Cincinnati, 1970.

Baker, William. "Mark Twain in Cincinnati: A Mystery Most Compelling." *American Literary Realism* 12, no. 2 (1979): 299–315.

Brammer, Mauck. "Winthrop B. Smith: Creator of the Eclectic Educational Series." *Ohio History* 80 (1971): 45–59.

Brown, Dale Patrick. *Brilliance and Balderdash: Early Lectures at Cincinnati's Mercantile Library.* Cincinnati: Mercantile Library, 2007.

Chambrun, Clara Longworth. *The Making of Nicholas Longworth.* New York: Bramwell Press, 1933.

Clubbe, John. *Cincinnati Observed: Architecture and History.* Columbus: Ohio State University Press, 1992.

Dickens, Charles. *American Notes.* Greenwich, CT: Fawcett, 1961.

Ferguson, Alfred R. "Charles Dickens in Ohio." *Ohio History* 59, no. 1 (1950): 14–25.

Foote, John P. *Memoirs of the Life of Samuel E. Foote.* Cincinnati: Robert Clarke, 1860.

Ford, Harvey S. "Thomas Buchanan Read and the Civil War: The Story of Sheridan's Ride." *Ohio History* 56, no. 3 (1947): 215–27.

Giglierano, Geoffrey J., and Deborah A. Overmyer. *The Bicentennial Guide to Greater Cincinnati: A Portrait of Two Hundred Years.* Cincinnati: Cincinnati Historical Society, 1988.

Goodman, Susan. *William Dean Howells: A Writer's Life.* Berkeley: University of California Press, 2005.

Gould, George M. *Concerning Lafcadio Hearn.* Philadelphia: George W. Jacobs, 1908.

Greve, Charles Theodore. *Centennial History of Cincinnati and Representative Citizens.* 2 vols. Chicago: Biographical, 1904.

Haffenden, John. *The Life of John Berryman.* Boston: Routledge and Kegan Paul, 1981.

Hagedorn, Ann. *Beyond the River: The Untold Story of the Heroes of the Underground Railroad.* New York: Simon and Schuster, 2002.

Hamilton, Ian. *Robert Lowell: A Biography.* New York: Random House, 1982.

Hedrick, Joan D. *Harriet Beecher Stowe: A Life.* New York: Oxford University Press, 1994.

Hillier, Bevis. *John Betjeman: New Fame, New Love.* London: John Murray, 2002.

Howells, William Dean. *Years of My Youth, and Three Essays.* Bloomington: Indiana University Press, 1975.

Hughes, Jon Christopher. *The Tanyard Murder: On the Case with Lafcadio Hearn.* Washington: University Press of America, 1982.

Hurst, Fannie. *Anatomy of Me: A Wonderer in Search of Herself.* Garden City, NY: Doubleday, 1958.

Hutchisson, James M. "'All of Us Americans at 46': The Making of Sinclair Lewis' *Babbitt.*" In *George F. Babbitt,* edited by Harold Bloom. Philadelphia: Chelsea House, 2004.

Kroeger, Brooke. *Fannie: The Talent for Success of Writer Fannie Hurst.* New York: Times Books, 1999.

Lewis, Sinclair. *Babbitt.* San Diego: Harcourt, Brace, 1922.

Lueders, Jeffrey R. "George Elliston's Meeting Place for Poets." *Cincinnati Horizons* 11, no. 1 (1981): 31–33.

Mansfield, Edward D. *Memoirs of the Life and Services of Daniel Drake, M.D.* Cincinnati: Applegate, 1855.

Marks, Andrew R. *The Rabbi and the Poet: Victor Reichert and Robert Frost.* Alton, NH: Andover Green, 1994.

Neville-Sington, Pamela. *Fanny Trollope: The Life and Adventures of a Clever Woman.* New York: Viking, 1998.

Newstedt, J. Roger. "Frances Trollope in Cincinnati: The 'Infernal Regions' and the Bizarre Bazaar, 1828–1830." *Queen City Heritage* 57, no. 4 (1999): 37–45.

———, ed. *The Literary Club of Cincinnati, 1849–1999*. Cincinnati: Literary Club of Cincinnati, 2001.

Parini, Jay. *Robert Frost: A Life*. New York: Henry Holt, 1999.

Peeke, Hewson L. "Charles Dickens in Ohio in 1842." *Ohio History* 28, no. 1 (1919): 72–81.

Pollitt, Ronald. *Helen Steiner Rice: Ambassador of Sunshine*. Grand Rapids, MI: F. H. Revell, 1994.

Potter, Eliza. *A Hairdresser's Experience in High Life*. Edited by Xiomara Santamarina. Chapel Hill: University of North Carolina Press, 2009.

Rice, Helen Steiner. *In the Vineyard of the Lord*. Old Tappan, NJ: F. H. Revell, 1979.

Smith, William E. *About the McGuffeys: William Holmes McGuffey and Alexander H. McGuffey*. Oxford, OH: Typoprint, 1967.

Stowe, Harriet Beecher. *The Key to Uncle Tom's Cabin*. Salem, NH: Ayer, 1987.

———. *The Mayflower and Miscellaneous Writings*. Boston: Phillips, Sampson, 1855.

Trollope, Frances Milton. *Domestic Manners of the Americans*. Edited by Donald Smalley. New York: Knopf, 1949.

Tucker, Louis L. "The Semi-Colon Club of Cincinnati." *Ohio History* 73 (1965): 13–26.

Venable, W. H. *Beginnings of Literary Culture in the Ohio Valley: Historical and Biographical Sketches*. Cincinnati: R. Clarke, 1891.

Vitz, Robert C. *At the Center: 175 Years at Cincinnati's Mercantile Library*. Cincinnati: Mercantile Library, 2010.

———. *The Queen and the Arts: Cultural Life in Nineteenth-Century Cincinnati*. Kent: Kent State University Press, 1989.

Westerhoff, John H. *McGuffey and His Readers: Piety, Morality, and Education in Nineteenth-Century America*. Nashville: Abingdon, 1978.

INDEX

Page numbers in italics refer to illustrations.

Viereck, Peter, 152

Walker, Timothy, 11, 31, 64, 69, 71–72, 172n8
Wallace, Lew, 47
Walters, Raymond, 125, 128, 154
Western Female Institute, 22, 38
Western Monthly Review, 6, 13
Western Museum, 4, 9, 16, 162n16

White, Edmund, 9, 159
Whittier, John Greenleaf, 51, 54, 55, 56
Wilson, Obed J., 42, 43
Wright, Fanny, 1, 4, 9
Wrightson and Company, 80, 81, 82, *83*

Young Men's Mercantile Library Association. *See* Mercantile Library of Cincinnati